Summer Fit Activities™

Sixth to Seventh Grade

Build Fit Brains and Fit Bodies!

 Fun, skill based activities in reading, writing, mathematics, and language arts with additional activities in science and geography. Curriculum activities are based on national standards.

 Summer Fitness program includes aerobic and strength exercises.. Fitness log, exercise videos and instructions included. Keeping young bodies active and strong helps children live better, learn more and feel healthier.

 Incentive Contract Calendars motivate children to complete activities and exercises by rewarding their efforts. Summer Explorers are lists of fun and active things to do — perfect for when your child says, "I'm bored, what can I do?"

 Core values and role model activities include child activities, parent talking points and reading lists.

 Summer Journaling, Book Reports, Health and Nutrition Index, Certificate of Completion and Flashcards.

Access more summer resou~~~~~~~~~
www.SummerFitActi~~~~~

D1411303

Written by: Veronica Brand

Fitness and Nutrition: Lisa Roberts RN, BSN, PHN, Coach James Cordova and Charles Miller

Cover Illustration: Amanda Sorensen

Illustrations: Roxanne Ottley, Amanda Sorensen

Page Layout: Robyn Pettit

For orders or product information call 801-466-4272

Dedication

Summer Fit™ is dedicated to Julia Hobbs and Carla Fisher who are the original authors of Summer Bridge Activities™. Julia and Carla helped pioneer summer learning and dedicated their lives to their vocation of teaching.

Caution

Exercises may require adult supervision. If you have any concerns regarding your child's ability to complete any of the suggested fitness activities, consult your family doctor or pediatrician. Children should always stretch and warm up before exercises. Do not push children past comfort level or ability. Exercises were created to be fun for parents and caregivers as well as the child, but not as a professional training or weight loss program. Exercise should stop immediately if you or your child experiences any of the following symptoms: pain, feeling dizzy or faint, nausea, or severe fatigue.

Copyright

ISBN 978-0-9982902-7-0

Table of Contents

Parent Section

Build Fit Brains & Fit Bodies I

Dear Parents IV

Inside Summer Fit™ V

Hints for Summer Fit™ VI

Summer Reading & Writing VII

Parents - Key & Tip VIII

Living Earth Friendly IX

Summer Fitness Program X

Summer Skills Review

Math & Reading 1-4

Activities and Exercises

Section 1

◆ Incentive Contract Calendar 5

▲ Fitness Log 6

★ Academic Activities, Days 1-4 7-14

● Honesty Value, Day 5 15-16

◆ Summer Explorer 17

■ Summer Journal 18

★ Academic Activities, Days 6-9 19-26

● Compassion Value, Day 10 27-28

Section 2

◆ Incentive Contract Calendar 29

▲ Fitness Log 30

★ Academic Activities, Days 1-4 31-38

● Trustworthiness Value, Day 5 39-40

◆ Summer Explorer 41

■ Summer Journal 42

★ Academic Activities, Days 6-9 43-50

● Self Discipline Value, Day 10 51-52

Section 3

◆ Incentive Contract Calendar 53

▲ Fitness Log 54

★ Academic Activities, Days 1-4 55-62

● Kindness Value, Day 5 63-64

◆ Summer Explorer 65

■ Summer Journal 66

★ Academic Activities, Days 6-9 67-74

● Courage Value, Day 10 75-76

Section 4

◆ Incentive Contract Calendar 77

▲ Fitness Log 78

★ Academic Activities, Days 1-4 79-86

● Respect Value, Day 5 87-88

◆ Summer Explorer 89

■ Summer Journal 90

★ Academic Activities, Days 6-9 91-98

● Responsibility Value, Day 10 99-100

Section 5

◆ Incentive Contract Calendar 101

▲ Fitness Log 102

★ Academic Activities, Days 1-4 103-110

● Perseverance Value, Day 5 111-112

◆ Summer Explorer 113

■ Summer Journal 114

★ Academic Activities, Days 6-9 115-122

● Friendship Value, Day 10 123-124

Extras

◆ Answer Pages 125-130

■ Book Reports 131-134

▲ Fitness Index 135-150

★ Flashcards . . . . A

Certificate of Completion . . . . P

★ = Academic   ● = Core Value   ▲ = Fitness   ■ = Writing   ◇ = Play & Do   ◆ = Track

Dear Parent,

As a mother, I value giving my children the academic resources they need for success in both their personal and school life. However, when summer comes it is hard to resist the urge to shutter the books and toss the backpacks in the closet.

I have learned first hand that the lack of study over the summer holiday can cause summer learning loss. Studies show that as much as 2.5 months of learning can be undone and some children have lower test scores during the period directly after summer. It is important to find a balance between summer vacation and homework. **Summer Fit Activities** is the resource that does it while looking and feeling like academic summer camp.

Summer Fit Activities is an engaging workbook that helps your child learn and grow. It contains three different foundation pieces for your child's success: academics, health, and values that help children become kinder, more empathetic and stronger leaders. **Summer Fit Activities** makes learning fun with colorful illustrations, family activities, fitness logs, and incentive calendars. Summer Fit is easy to use for parents, caregivers and even grandparents, because day-by-day lesson plans are straightforward and flexible to allow you to create a summer learning experience specifically for your child.

Summer Fit Activities educates the whole child just like you would in summer camp- with an emphasis on FUN. My children love the healthy snack ideas they can make on their own and the Summer Explorer lists of outdoor learning activities that provide hands on learning experiences. I love the flashcards included in the back of book to help reinforce basic skills and the peace of mind knowing that I am teaching my child to be a great person, as well as a great student.

Summer is a time for adventure and fun, but it is also a time of learning and growth. With **Summer Fit Activities** I found the balance I was looking for - unplug, learn and let the magic of summer unfold before your eyes!

Have a wonderful summer,

Christa
Parent

INSIDE
Summer Fit Activities™

Here is what you will find inside Summer Fit™:

Academics

- There are 5 sections of academic exercises, each section with its own core value and journal entry page.

- Sections begin with Incentive Contract Calendars and "Summer Fitness Logs."

- Your child will complete activities in reading, writing, math and language arts. Science and geography activities are included throughout the book.

- When your child completes each day, he/she may color or initial the academic and reading icon for that day on the Incentive Contract Calendar.

- Parents initial the Incentive Contract Calendar once the section has been completed.

Fitness

Research shows that keeping bodies strong and healthy helps children learn better, live better and even miss fewer days of school! To keep bodies healthy, children need to eat right, get enough sleep and exercise daily.

- The Summer Fitness Program helps children set goals and track performance over the summer.

- Daily aerobic and strength exercises

- Fitness & Health Index includes Nutrition page, Foods to Eat Everyday & Meal Tracker.

- Online videos show the proper way to complete exercises.

Values Education

Core values are fundamental to society and are incorporated into our civil laws. Research shows that character education is more effective when parents encourage values in their child's daily routine. Core values are vitally important to the overall growth, well-being and success of all children.

- Each section highlights two different values and role models.

- Value activities are designed for children and parents.

- Each value includes a reading comprehension activity based on role models from throughout the world.

Helpful Hints for Summer Fit™

1 Flip through the book to become familiar with the layout and activities. Look ahead to the upcoming core value so you can incorporate discussions and activities into your daily routine.

2 Provide your child with the tools he/she will need to complete the work: pencils, pens, crayons, ruler, and healthy dose of encouragement.

3 Try to set aside a specific time to do Summer Fit™ each day (for example, after breakfast each morning). Make sure your child has enough time to complete the day's work and exercise.

4 Be a cheerleader! Encourage your child to do their best, urging them to challenge themselves. Make sure they know you are there to help them if they need support. Talk about and reinforce the material in the book beyond the page. For example, after reading about insects, encourage your child to find an insect in the yard to observe and draw.

5 Look at your child's work frequently. Make sure they know you value what they are doing and it is not just "busywork".

6 Try doing Summer Fit™ outside in the fresh air: at the park, in the backyard, camping, or on the beach. Summer Fit™ can go wherever you go!

7 Ask older siblings, grandparents, babysitters and even friends to participate in and give one on one help with the activities. Summer Fit™ is great shared experience!

8 Keep up with the Incentive Contract Calendars. Follow through and reward completed work: stamps, stickers, hugs, and high fives are great ways to motivate and recognize a job well done.

9 Let your child do more than one page at a sitting if he/she is enthusiastic and wants to work ahead. Make sure to check the website for additional activities and resources that can help you tailor Summer Fit™ to your child's needs.

10 When the book has been completed, display the Certificate of Completion proudly and let your child know what a great job he/she did. Celebrate!

Encourage Summer Reading and Writing

Reading and writing skills are important skills for your child's success. Summer is a great time to encourage and build reading and writing skills with your child regardless of ability.

You can do many things to encourage literacy and writing:

 Make Reading a Priority: Create a routine by establishing a reading time each day for your child.

 Read Around Your Child: Read in front of him/her as much as possible. Talk with your child about the books you are reading.

 Create a Summer Reading List: Find books that involve your child's favorite interests like sports, art, mysteries, dance, etc.

 Reading On The Road: Billboards, menus, street signs, window banners and packaging labels are great ways to reinforce reading comprehension skills.

 Storytelling: Have campfire nights in your backyard and tell stories about things you did when you were their age. Slip in a few scary spooks as well!

 Read Together: Newspapers, magazine articles and stories on the Internet are great to read together and discuss.

 Library Time: Go to the library on a weekly basis to choose new books.

 Letter Writing: Encourage your child to write thank you notes and letters.

 Plan a Trip: Have your child plan a trip for the family. Have him/her write an overview of the trip including where, what to bring, how to travel, how long and what you will do on your trip.

 Create a Joke Book: Provide a list of subjects for your child to create jokes about.

 Family Writing Hour: Sit down as a family and write a story together. Read the story out loud at the end.

 Script Writing: Ask your child to write a movie script. When it is finished, perform it as a family – be sure to video the production!

 Poetry: Discuss different forms of poetry. Have your child write a poem. Add an illustration.

Mindfulness

As a parent or guardian it is easy to get pulled into the many distractions of daily life. Have you ever wondered if your child has the same difficulties juggling personal interests with school with all the beeps, phone calls and text messages along the way?

Multitasking, compounded with technology, can make it difficult for all of us to concentrate on what we are doing in the moment. Growing research shows that we are hard wired to focus on one thing at a time. Teaching your child to be mindful and to focus on their internal feelings allows your child to fully experience what they are doing in the moment and can have a lasting effect on what, how and why they learn. Learning to sit without distractions and to focus on the moment is a gradual process that has immense benefits for you and your child.

Parent Tips to Help Children Be Mindful

 Time Set a time when all noises, distractions and devices are turned off — start with 5 minutes a day.

 Talk Ask your child to clear her thoughts and to focus on not thinking about anything.

 Focus Focus on breathing, take deep breathes and exhale slowly.

 Quiet Sit in silence.

 Show Show your child gratitude by thanking her for her time. Ask her what she is thankful for and discuss the importance of being grateful.

Living Earth Friendly

We all share this home called Earth, and each one of us needs to be responsible in helping take care of her. There are many things families can do together to REDUCE, REUSE, and RECYCLE in order to be kind to Mother Earth. We can all BE SMART AND DO OUR PART!

There are many opportunities each day for us to practice these little steps with our children and we should talk with them about how little things add up to make a big impact.

REDUCE, REUSE, RECYCLE

REDUCE: Means to use less of something. Encourage your children to use water wisely, turn off lights when leaving a room, and use your own bags at the grocery store.

REUSE: Means to use an item again. Refill water bottles, wash dishes and containers instead of using disposable, mend or repair the things you have before buying new, and donate clothes and toys to be used by someone else.

RECYCLE: Means to make a new thing out of an old one. Recycle cans, bottles, and newspapers. Participate in local environmental initiatives like recycling drives.

REBUY: Means to purchase items that have already been used or recycled. Shop at thrift and consignment stores and when possible buy items that have been made from recycled materials.

6-7 • © Summer Fit Activities™

Summer Fitness Program

Choose a strength or cardio exercise for each day of academic activities. Check the box ✓ each day you complete your fitness activity. Fill in the Fitness Log on the back of each Incentive Contract Calendar. Choose exercises from the Health and Nutrition section in the back of the book. Exercise videos can be viewed at **www.SummerFitActivities.com.**

	Date	Stretch	Activity	Time
1.	*examples:* June 4	Run in place	Sky Reach	7 min
2.	June 5	Toe Touches	Bottle Curls	15 min
3.				
4.				
5.				

Let's Move!

Warm Up! Get ready to exercise by stretching and moving around.

Stretch! Move your head slowly side to side, try to touch each shoulder. Now move your head forward, touch your chin to your chest, then look up and as far back as you can. Try to touch your back with the back of your head.

Touch your toes when standing. Bend over at the waist and touch the end of your toes or the floor. Hold this position for 10 seconds.

Move! Walk or jog in place for 3-5 minutes to warm up before you exercise. Shake your arms and roll your shoulders when you are finished.

Find out where your child needs a little extra practice!

1.
```
  5319
  8374
  3268
+ 1258
```
18219

2.
```
  0.48
  2.23
+ 1.99
```
4.70

3.
```
  876
- 169
```
707

4. 2306 + 3217 + 9335 = *14,858*

5. 2341 − 87 = *2,254*

6. 785.32 − 45.8 = *739.52*

7.
```
  57.29
- 2.376
```
54.914

8.
```
  239
x  72
```

9.
```
  408
x 257
```

10. 519 x 67 = *34,572*

11. 8.2 x 19 = *155.8*

12. 41 x 8.3 = *340.3*

13. 641 x 2.76 + = *1759.16*

14.
```
   87
x 9.1
```
791.7

15.
```
  2.5
x 7.3
```
18.25

16.
```
  4.18
x  927
```
3874.86

17. 8 ⟌ 696

18. 24 ⟌ 1704

19. 8 ⟌ 34

20. 1.5 ⟌ 55.5

21. 22 ⟌ 119 .02

22. 7.6 ⟌ 397.48

23. What is the Greatest Common Factor of 42 and 12?

24. What is the Least Common Multiple of 2, 3, and 5?
30

25. Circle the two equivalent fractions. $\frac{3}{12}$ $\frac{1}{12}$ $\frac{1}{3}$ $\frac{1}{4}$

26. Which fraction in each pair is larger?   a. $\frac{5}{6}$ $\frac{7}{12}$ b. $\frac{1}{6}$ $\frac{4}{15}$ c. $\frac{3}{4}$ $\frac{2}{3}$

$\frac{3}{30}$

27. Change the mixed number to a mixed fraction. $5\frac{1}{3}$ $\frac{15}{3}$

28. Add the fractions.

a. $\frac{2}{5} + \frac{1}{5} = \frac{3}{5}$

b. $\frac{5}{8} + \frac{3}{4} = \frac{11}{8} = 1\frac{3}{8}$

c. $7\frac{1}{5} + 3\frac{2}{3} = 10\frac{13}{15}$

29. Subtract the fractions.

a. $\frac{4}{5} - \frac{1}{5} = \frac{3}{5}$

b. $\frac{11}{15} - \frac{3}{5} = \frac{2}{15}$

c. $8\frac{4}{5} - 3\frac{4}{15} = 5\frac{8}{15}$

Multiply the fractions.

30. $\frac{2}{3} \times \frac{4}{5} = \frac{8}{15}$

31. $3\frac{3}{2} \times 5\frac{3}{5} = \frac{9}{2} \times \frac{28}{5} = \frac{96}{5}$

Divide the fractions.

32. $\frac{4}{3} \div \frac{2}{9} = 6$

$\frac{4}{3} \times \frac{9}{2} = \frac{12}{2} = 6$

33. $6 \div \frac{6}{7} = 7$

$6 \times \frac{7}{6}$

Solve the proportion.

34. $\frac{6}{7} = \frac{n}{14} = 12$

35. $\frac{5}{8} \div \frac{a}{24} = 3$

$\frac{5}{8} \times \frac{24}{5} = 3$

36. $\frac{67}{100}$ 67 %

37. $40\% = \frac{2}{5}$

$\frac{40}{100} = \frac{20}{50} = \frac{2}{5}$

38. $0.43 = 43$ %

Match the following genres of literature with the phrase which best describes it.

1. _C_ historical fiction   a. a story which may take place in the future
2. _a_ science fiction   b. a story about a real person written by another person
3. _f_ fantasy   c. a story which places fictional characters in a historical setting
4. _b_ biography   d. a story with make believe creatures
5. _g_ autobiography   e. an essay or story which is not made up
6. _d_ myth   f. a story which may have a moral or teach a lesson
7. _h_ mystery   g. a story about a person written by themself
8. _e_ non-fiction   h. a story where a person may try to solve a crime

Match the following literary terms with their description.

1. _C_ setting   a. the high point of a story
2. _b_ sequence   b. the order of events in a story
3. _e_ plot   c. time and place in which a story is set
4. _a_ climax   d. exaggeration
5. _d_ hyperbole   e. a brief summary of a story

6. _b_ idiom   a. a direct comparison of two unlike things
7. _C_ metaphor   b. a comparison of two unlike things using "like" or "as"
8. _a_ simile   c. a phrase having a literal meaning and a figurative one
9. _e_ personification   d. an expression not to be taken literally
10. _d_ pun   e. attributing a non-human thing with human characteristics

11. _b_ irony   a. repetition of vowel sounds in a phrase or sentence
12. ___ alliteration   b. saying one thing but meaning another
13. ___ assonance   c. words near each other beginning with the same letter
14. _e_ rhyme   d. word whose name suggests the sound it makes
15. ___ onomatopoeia   e. words which end in the same sound

16. _d_ moral   a. the viewpoint from which a story is told
17. _e_ synonym   b. two words with opposite meanings
18. _b_ antonym   c. the pattern of rhyme found in a poem
19. _a_ perspective   d. lesson to be learned from a story
20. _C_ rhyme scheme   e. two words with the same meaning

It was cold. There was no sign of grass, just white as far as the eye could see. The sky was a clear, sparkling blue. Even the blue looked cold. But, Erika didn't mind the cold. She was bundled up warmly. She even had hand warmers inside her plush mittens and some warmers in her boots. The only part of her really exposed to the cold was the horn that protruded from her forehead. It was blue, too, because that was its normal color, but she did feel the cold through the horn. Still, cold had always been part of Erica's life, and she didn't mind it.

1. This story is probably (a. a biography)   b. a fantasy   c. non-fiction

2. What in the story tells you this? _It tells about Erika's life... for example 'Cold has always been part Erika's life'._

3. What season is Erika experiencing?   a. spring   b. fall   (c. winter)

4. Cite two phrases from the story which tell you what season it is. _One cite from the text is 'there was no sighn of grass, just white as far as the eye could see.' Another example from the text is, 'She was bundled up warmly.'_

INCENTIVE CONTRACT CALENDAR

My parents and I agree that if I complete this section of

Summer Fit Activities™

and read _____ minutes a day, my reward will be _____

Child Signature: _____   Parent Signature: _____

Day 1			Day 6		
Day 2			Day 7		
Day 3			Day 8		
Day 4			Day 9		
Day 5			Day 10		

Color the for each day of activities completed.

Color the for each day of reading completed.

Summer Fitness Log

Choose your exercise activity each day from the Aerobic and Strength Activities in the back of the book. Record the date, stretch, activity and how long you performed your exercise activity below. Fill in how many days you complete your fitness activity on your Incentive Contract Calendars.

	Date	Stretch	Activity	Time
examples:	June 4	Run in place	Sky Reach	7 min
	June 5	Toe Touches	Bottle Curls	15 min
1.				
2.				
3.				
4.				
5.				
6.				
7.				
8.				
9.				
10.				

I promise to do my best for me. I exercise to be healthy and active. I am awesome because I am me.

Child Signature: _____

Science - Cell Parts

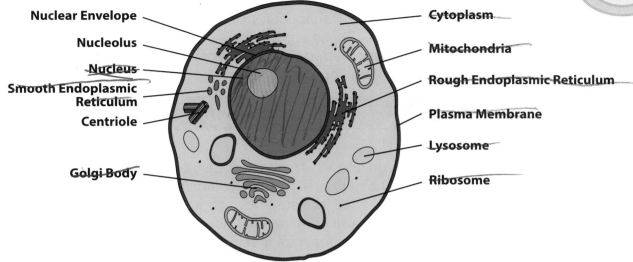

Nuclear Envelope
Nucleolus
Nucleus
Smooth Endoplasmic Reticulum
Centriole
Golgi Body

Cytoplasm
Mitochondria
Rough Endoplasmic Reticulum
Plasma Membrane
Lysosome
Ribosome

All living things on earth are made up of cells.

A cell is surrounded by a thin wall called a membrane. Inside the membrane is a clear gel called cytoplasm. Cytoplasm contains proteins, amino acids, sugars, vitamins, ions, fatty acids and nucleotides. There are several parts to the cell. Mitochondrion produces the major portion of cell energy. The lysosome is a special digestive compartment. The Golgi Body is where proteins are put together to be sent to other parts of the cell. The smooth and rough endoplasmic reticulum are a system of membranes where proteins are synthesized. A ribosome is where protein chains are synthesized. Most ribosomes are attached to the outside of the endoplasmic reticulum, but some are free in the cytoplasm. The nucleus contains genetic material. This is where DNA is stored and replicated.

1. The nucleolus is inside the ___nucleus___ .

2. Two elements of the animal cell not mentioned in the paragraph are

___nucleolus___ and ___nuclear envenlope___ .

Adding four digit numbers

1.	2.	3.	4.	5.
6,238	5,916	2,730	9,146	8,095
2,085	3,618	3,567	9,217	4,107
3,419	2,430	9,184	8,350	3,268
1,973	8,194	7,421	3,863	6,440
+ 4,510	+ 2,105	+ 1,606	+ 2,584	+ 5,286
18,325	22,263	24,508	33,160	27,196

6. 2,306 + 4,165 + 7,839 = 15,210

7. 7,745 + 6,201 + 9,335 = 22,281

8. 5,026 + 7,139 + 7,835 = 22,891

A noun names a person, place, or thing. Most nouns are easy to recognize – they are things you can point at, see, or touch. These are things like desk, dog, car. Other nouns are invisible. These are ideas like freedom, hatred, intelligence. They seem tricky at first, but are actually easy. Here is a strategy to help you identify them. Look at these words:

happy	liberty	stupid

Liberty is the only noun. How do you know? There is an easy test which tells you. Ask yourself, "Can I have it?" Can you have happy, No, but you can have happiness or joy. They're nouns. Can you have stupid? No, but stupidity, ignorance, intolerance – all these you can have. This test works because all of these idea nouns are things, and you can have things. Idea nouns are really thing nouns, they are just invisible things.

From the list below, circle the words which are nouns.

honesty	sad	honest	brave
charm	integrity	bravery	courage
funny	humor	kindness	mean
charity	fear	scared	hope
interesting	clever	angry	anger
talented	talent	childish	innocence
nervous	confidence	worried	manners

Choose your STRENGTH exercise!

Day 1

Exercise for today:

Check & Record in Fitness Log.

Mesopotamia

Find these major cities and circle each one on map:

Assur

Babylon

Nineveh

Phoenicia

Sumer

Ur

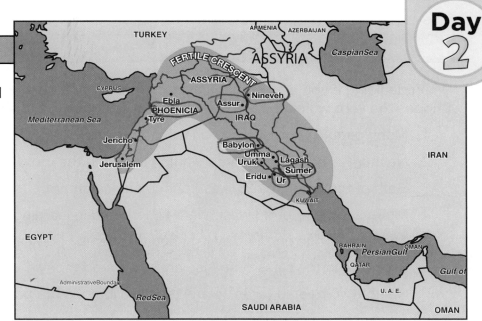

Many early civilizations grew around water sources. Water was important for growing crops as well as providing hydration for people and animals. One of the earliest civilizations began in the area known as the Fertile Crescent. This area is between two rivers, the Tigris and the Euphrates. In fact, the name Mesopotamia in Greek means "the land between two rivers."

Today, the Fertile Crescent includes the countries of Iraq, Syria, Lebanon, Cyprus, Jordan, Palestine, Kuwait, the Sinai Peninsula, and Northern Mesopotamia. It is a big place.

Adding four digit numbers

1.
```
    0.48
    0.17
  + 0.32
  _____
    0.97
```

2.
```
    9.00
   17.87
  + 3.65
  _____
   29.52
```

3.
```
   14.14
    9.82
  + 0.28
  _____
   24.24
```

4.
```
   23.62
   10.62
  + 4.75
  _____
   38.99
```

5.
```
   46.09
    3.99
 + 22.78
  _____
   72.66
```

6. 52.94 + 16.07 = 69.03

7. 0.821 + 0.976 + 1.088 = 2.885

8. 37.62 + 0.976 = 38.596

9. 0.09 + 5.027 + 23.784 = 28.891

10. 324.9 + 28 + 14.006 = 366.906

```
  324.900
  028.000
  014.006
  _____
  366.906
```

```
   37.620
 + 00.976
  _____
   38.596
```

```
   0.821
   0.976
 + 1.088
  _____
   2.885
```

```
  0 0.090
  0 5.027
 + 23.784
  _____
   28.891
```

When deciding if you are using the correct verb form, it helps to read the sentence aloud.
Choose the verb which agrees with the noun or nouns in the sentence. Circle your choice.

1. Many people (agree , agrees) with my opinion.
2. Neither Bill nor Jose (want , wants) to watch the movie.
3. Both of the boys (like , likes) chocolate ice cream.
4. Moira and her friend (was , were) interested in learning to knit.
5. All of the songs on the play list (seem , seems) popular.
6. Everyone in the classroom (is , are) prepared today.
7. Ninety-two people (was , were) ready to jump in the pool.
8. Several of the books that were on sale (appeals, appeal) to me.
9. The big striped cat (don't , doesn't) like to sit in my lap.
10. George and Tatyana (don't , doesn't) come to this restaurant.
11. Either the boy or his sister (play , plays) in the band.
12. All the students (claps , clap) when the teacher declares a no homework day.
13. Anna Maria (was , were) dressed for a party.
14. The dogs in the neighborhood (bark , barks) at my cat.
15. The picture in the front hallway (hang , hangs) crookedly.

Subtraction Review

1. 876 - 234 642	2. 678 - 432 246	3. 237 - 156 81	4. 715 - 428 287	5. 6,254 - 193 6061

6. $2,342 - 961 = 1,381$

7. $9,228 - 1,417 = 7,811$

8. $6,247 - 96 = 6,151$

$$\begin{array}{r} 2342 \\ -\ 961 \\ \hline 1381 \end{array}$$

$$\begin{array}{r} 9228 \\ -1417 \\ \hline 7811 \end{array}$$

$$\begin{array}{r} 6247 \\ -\ 96 \\ \hline 6151 \end{array}$$

Choose your AEROBIC exercise!

Exercise for today:

Check & Record in Fitness Log.

Day 2

Characteristics of Jo Marsh from Little Women

We usually get to know a person slowly, over time, but an author has to let you get to know a character very quickly. When we get to know someone we pay attention to what they look like, how they act, what they say. We also pay attention to what others say about them. These are some of the same methods reader use to learn about character traits, or qualities. In a story, look for clues to a character's personality and qualities by paying attention to several things:

The thoughts, feelings, actions and speech of the character
The thoughts, feelings, actions and speech of other characters
What the writer says directly about the character
The character's physical description

Read the following selection from Little Women, by Louisa May Alcott.

"Jo does use such slang words!" observed Amy, with a
reproving look at the long figure stretched on the rug.
Jo immediately sat up, put her hands in her pockets, and
began to whistle.
"Don't, Jo. It's so boyish!"
"That's why I do it."
"I detest rude, unladylike girls!"
"I hate affected, niminy-piminy chits!"
"Birds in their little nests agree," sang Beth, the
peacemaker, with such a funny face that both sharp voices
softened to a laugh, and the "pecking" ended for that time.
"Really, girls, you are both to be blamed," said Meg,
beginning to lecture in her elder-sisterly fashion. "You are old
enough to leave off boyish tricks, and to behave better,
Josephine. It didn't matter so much when you were a little
girl, but now you are so tall, and turn up your hair, you should
remember that you are a young lady."
"I'm not! And if turning up my hair makes me one, I'll
wear it in two tails till I'm twenty," cried Jo, pulling off
her net, and shaking down a chestnut mane. "I hate to think
I've got to grow up, and be Miss March, and wear long gowns,
and look as prim as a China Aster! It's bad enough to be a
girl, anyway, when I like boy's games and work and manners! I
can't get over my disappointment in not being a boy. And it's
worse than ever now, for I'm dying to go and fight with Papa.
And I can only stay home and knit, like a poky old woman!"

1. How does Jo feel about behaving like a lady? Cite 2 phrases from the story to support your claim.

_____

_____

_____

2. What does Jo do to act like a boy? _____

_____

Plant cells compared to animal cells

Plant and animal cells have many similarities. They both have Cytoplasm, Endoplasmic Reticulum, and Ribosomes. Both have Mitochondria, Golgi Apparatus, and a nucleus.

There are differences, too. Animal cells do not have a cell wall, chloroplasts, or plastids. Animal cells are generally round, with an irregular shape. Plant cells have a fixed rectangular shape. They both have vacuoles, but those in animal cells are much smaller than the one large vacuole of a plant cell. Centrioles are present in all animal cells, but only lower plant form cells. Animal cells have only a cell membrane, plant cells have a cell wall and a cell membrane. Cilia are present in animal cells, but rarely in plant cells.

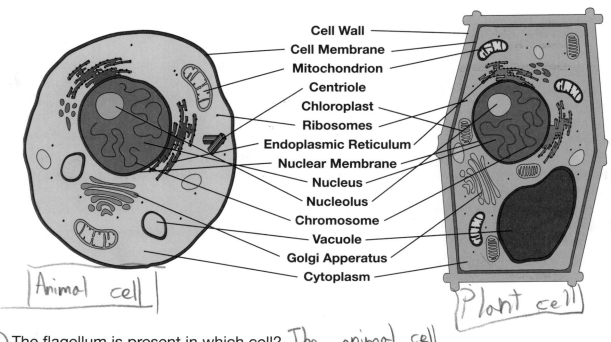

Cell Wall
Cell Membrane
Mitochondrion
Centriole
Chloroplast
Ribosomes
Endoplasmic Reticulum
Nuclear Membrane
Nucleus
Nucleolus
Chromosome
Vacuole
Golgi Apperatus
Cytoplasm

Animal cell

Plant cell

1. The flagellum is present in which cell? _The animal cell_
2. The thicker cell wall is present in which cell? _The plant cell_
3. Which cell has the larger vacuole? _The plant cell_
4. Name two differences between the plant and the animal cell. _The plant cell has a_ _cell wall and the animal cell has a more round, and_ _plant cells are more in a rectangular shape_

Choose your STRENGTH exercise!

Exercise for today:

Day 3

Check & Record in Fitness Log.

6–7 • ©Summer Fit Activities™

Children were very important to the Ancient Egyptians. If a family could not have children, they tried magic, praying to various gods and goddesses, even placing letters at the tombs of dead relatives. They thought the relatives who were dead could possibly influence the gods. If nothing else worked, they might adopt a child.

Children were important because they carried on the life of the family. The boys would learn their father's trade. Girls would learn from their mothers how to run a house. Boys from wealthier families could also go to school. They learned religion, reading, writing and arithmetic.

Children were also supposed to take care of their parents as they aged. When the parents died, the sons would inherit the land. The daughters would inherit the household goods such as furniture and jewelry. If there were no sons, the daughter could also inherit the land.

1. What did sons contribute to the family? _They would learn there father's trade._

2. What did girls learn to do? _They would learn how to run a house._

3. What was one way people would try to be sure they could have a child? _They would_
try magic, or praying to various gods and goddesses.

Subtract with decimals (Remember sometimes you need to add a zero for a place holder)

1. 7.26	2. 23.87	3. 67.18	4. 263.1	5. 201.81
- 1.14	- 1.6	- 9.236	- 5.29	- 160.78
6.12	22.70	78.56	257.89	41.03

6. 863.14 – 621.7 = 241.44

7. 42.8 - 23.16 = 19.76

Multiplication practice

1. 672	2. 819	3. 725	4. 304	5. 738
x 56	x 23	x 40	x 972	x 605
4032	2457	29000	608	3690
+ 3360x	+1638x		2128x	+ 4428x
37632	18,837		+2736xx	478700
			295488	

6. 467 x 513 = 239,591

7. 709 x 76 = 53,884

A pronoun is a word used instead of a noun. Using the correct pronoun is an important skill. Circle the correct pronoun in each set of parentheses.

1. I brought James, Charlie and (she, her) to school.

2. Henry, Tom and (I , me) did not believe what John, Bill and (she , her) said.

3. Jaime and (I, me) do not know whether Frank, Ben, or (he , him) will come.

4. (They , Them) and the girls are following us.

5. It is (I , me), not (he , him), who am to blame for the torn picture.

6. (We , Us) students have done our very best.

7. Sarai gave the book to Jose and (he , him) gave it to (they , them).

8. Dan and (he , him), as well as Maria and (I , me) met Grace and (he , him).

9. (They , them) asked (I , me) to go with (they , them).

10. Gabrielle can't go with (he , him) and (she , her).

11. (He , Him) and (I , me) are going out to dinner.

12. The students and (I , me) are having a good day.

13. (We , Us) and (they , them) are playing the final match.

14. My father sent Therese and (I , me) a card.

15. The principal was staring at (they , them) and (we , us).

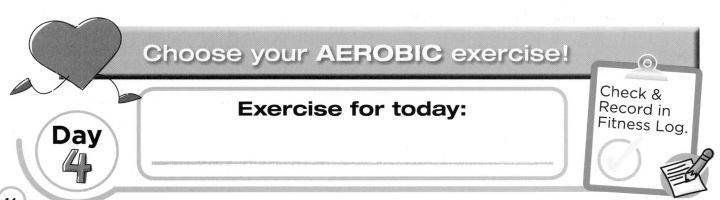

Choose your AEROBIC exercise!

Exercise for today:

Check & Record in Fitness Log.

Day 4

HONESTY

HONESTY - Essa Khan

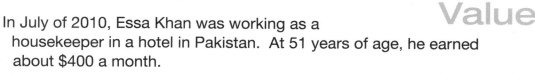

In July of 2010, Essa Khan was working as a housekeeper in a hotel in Pakistan. At 51 years of age, he earned about $400 a month.

A Japanese worker had been staying in the hotel, and when he left, Khan found $50,000 in the room. He immediately contacted the hotel manager, who got in touch with the guest. Kahn said he never considered keeping the money. He said, "Times are hard for everyone, but that doesn't mean we should start stealing and taking things which do not belong to us."

The Governor of Punjab held a ceremony at the Governor's mansion to honor this act of honesty. The story has appeared in newspapers throughout the world. The governor, in praising Khan, said that his honesty had earned fame for Pakistan throughout the world.

An award for honest employees of the Serena Hotels has been named after Khan. He has also been rewarded for his honesty.

---

1. What is the capital of Pakistan? _____

2. Who do you know that demonstrates honesty? How do they do this? My mom. She did because she told me we were going to get a dog one day, and we are right know looking for them

3. Why might it have been difficult for Kahn to give back the money he found? He was only getting $500 a month, and needed more money. $50,000 was a lot for him espacilly because it's $10,000 less then a year of his pay.

4. What did the Serena Hotels name after Kahn? An award of honest employees.

_____

Value:

HONESTY

Being honest means to be truthful in what you say and do. It means that you do not lie, cheat or steal. Sometimes this can be difficult, especially when we are scared or ashamed about something we did. Sometimes it takes courage to be honest, especially when it is uncomfortable.

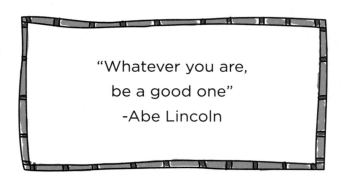

"Whatever you are,
be a good one"
-Abe Lincoln

What does honesty look like? Choose an honest action below and draw a picture to represent it in the picture frame.

- I cheat on a test.
- I keep a promise.
- I play fair.
- I take a candy bar from the store without paying.
- I take money out of my dad's wallet without asking.
- I find $5.00 at the library and take it to the front desk.

Please keep this a secret

no problem

he kept the secret!

How does it feel when someone lies to you?

Sad, depressed, irritated, annoyed, and very dissapointed.

Day 5

Choose a Play or Exercise Activity!

Summer Explorer
Healthy Planet Activities and Fun Things to Do!

- Visit the library and get a card if you do not have one.

- Make a biodegradable bird feeder and hang it in the yard.

- Play flashlight tag.

- Visit a fire station. Does your family have a plan of what to do in case of fire? Plan a family fire drill.

- Sign up for a free summer reading program at your local bookstore.

- Look up and find figures in the clouds.

- Play an outdoor game like "Simon Says" or "Kick the Can" with family or friends.

- Write a poem.

- Go for a bike ride.

- Pick up trash around your neighborhood and recycle.

- Find an ant colony. Drop some crumbs and observe what happens. Stay away from fire ants.

- Watch a sunrise or sunset, paint a picture of it.

- Make S'mores and tell ghost stories under the stars.

- Create an obstacle course. Invite your friends and time them to see how fast they complete it.

- Go for a walk.

Biodegradable Birdfeeder

 Collect your supplies: peanut butter, birdseed, oranges, and string for hanging.

 Tie a long string around the pinecone or toilet roll before spreading peanut butter on them and rolling in birdseed. Cut an orange in half, scoop out fruit and fill with birdseed. Attach strings to hang feeder in branch.

 Hang your bird treat in the yard and watch for your feathered friends to come and feast.

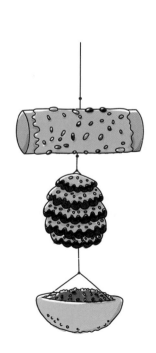

Summer Journal I

Write about your favorite outdoor summer activity.

Example: Camping, swimming or biking

Have you ever read the short explanation of a movie or TV show? That's a great example of how to write a plot summary. A plot summary can be a simple paragraph or a page or two, depending on the size of the piece and the amount of detail in the summary.

For example, for the movie *Night At The Museum*, you might read: A new night security guard at the Museum of Natural History realizes that an ancient curse causes the animals and exhibits on display to come to life and wreak havoc.

For the book *Where the Red Fern Grows*, you might read: A boy in the Ozarks wants desperately to buy two hound dogs, so that he can hunt. Despite family hardships and personal difficulties, Billy orders his dogs. He sneaks away from home to go into town to pick them up. Once he acquires the dogs, they all have a great series of adventures. He has to train the dogs, himself. His dad and grandpa give advice, but ultimately it is up to Billy. After many hunting trips, some close calls, and a tragic accident, Billy, his dad and grandpa take the dogs to a big championship hunt. Will they be able to compete against professionally trained, expensive dogs?

Choose a book you have read in the past year. Write a summary of at least 5 sentences. Be sure to cover the major plot points. Check your work for spelling and grammar correctness.

_____

_____

_____

_____

_____

_____

_____

_____

_____

Remember, when there is one decimal in the problem, there will be one decimal in your answer. Multiply as you normally would, then place the decimal to the left of the last number in your answer (thereby giving you one decimal in the answer).

1. 15
    x 2.3
    45
    + 30 x
    34.5

2. 96
    x 6.1
    96
    + 576 x
    585.6

3. 87
    x 4.5
    435
    + 348 x
    391.5

4. 43
    x 1.7
    301
    + 43 x
    73.1

5. 28
    x 3.5
    140
    + 84 x
    98.0

37
x 2.1
37
+ 74 x
77.7

6. 6.5
    x 7.1
    65
    + 455 x
    461.5

7. 8.3
    x 5.6
    498
    + 415 x
    46.48

8. 9.6
    x 4.7
    672
    + 384 x
    45.12

9. 2.5
    x 12
    50
    + 25 x
    300

10. 6.4
    x 7.5
    320
    + 558 x
    69.00

64
x 7.5
320
+ 448
480.0

11. 37 x 2.1 = 77.7

12. 64 x 7.5 = 480.

Greece

Greek houses, in the 6th and 5th century BCE, were made up of two or three rooms, built around an open air courtyard. Larger homes might also have a kitchen, a room for bathing, and perhaps a woman's sitting area.

Greek women were only allowed to leave their homes for short periods of time. The courtyard was a perfect place for them to enjoy the open air, in the privacy of their own home. In fact, the whole family made good use of the courtyard.

The ancient Greeks loved stories, myths and fables. The family would gather in the courtyard to hear these stories, told by the mother or father.

Meals were usually eaten in the courtyard. Greek cooking equipment was small and light and could easily be set up there. The heat was kept out of the home and the courtyard was visually enjoyable for the dining experience.

1. What claim can you make about the climate of Greece based on this selection?

That Greece was a very relaxing weather.

2. What type of furniture might you find in an open air courtyard?

chairs, a table, and an umbrellas

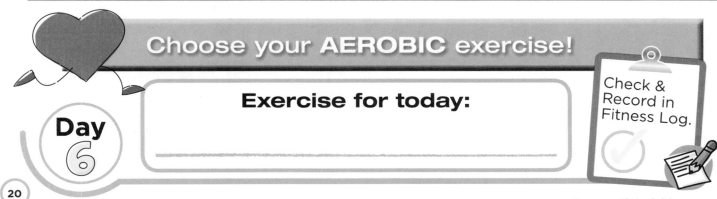

Choose your AEROBIC exercise!

Exercise for today:

Check & Record in Fitness Log.

Day 6

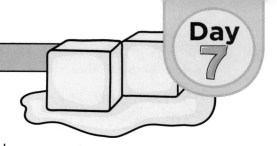

Conduction

When two objects come into contact with each other, heat energy moves between them because the particles in one object collide with, or 'bing,' the particles in the other object. Transferred heat resulting from the collision of particles is called conduction. Conduction works best through solids, especially through materials such as metals. An example includes observing a raw egg fry as it hits a heated frying pan.

Try this activity: Put an ice cube in a Ziploc bag. Make a prediction about how long it will take you to melt the ice cube by using only your hands. When you are finished, reflect on this question: did the ice make your hands cold or did the heat from your hands cause the ice to melt. Cite information below to support your reflection.

_____

_____

_____

_____

_____

_____

Multiply 3 digits by 3 digits, with 2 decimals

Remember, wherever the two decimals are in the problem does not matter. You still need to put two decimal places in your answer. You always move from the right, even if there is a zero at the end. (In multiplication, you don't have to line up decimals.)

1.
```
     508
  x 2.82
   1016
 + 4064 x
  1016 x x
 1432.56
```

2.
```
    247
  x 5.87
   1729
  1976 x
 1235 x x
 144989
```

3.
```
    247
  x 4.07
   1729
  1000 x
 + 988 x x
 1005.20
```

4.
```
    34.2
  x 28.2
   684
  2636 x
 + 684 x x
  954.44
```

5.
```
    6.42
  x 5 31
   642
  1926 x
 + 3210 x x
 3409.02
```

6. 632 x 1.23 =

7. 51.8 x 74.2 =

8. 3.29 x 167 =

- The dash is used to indicate a sudden or abrupt change in thought.
  Example: I will write the letter – but someone's at the door.

- The dash may be used to enclose material which could be in parenthesis.
  Example: Sometime next week – I forget when – I have an appointment.

- The dash is used before a word that sums up a preceding list of words.
  Example: English, mathematics, and science – these are important high school subjects.

Place dashes in the correct places in these sentence.

1. The boys need to pick up the trash–but the bell just rang.

2. I have five dollars in my–oh, no,–I think I left my wallet at home.

3. I would ask–or insist that you be quiet during the play.

4. Clothes, magazine, phone charger–all I need for my little trip is packed.

5. This is very important–are you listening to me?

6. I need three things to fix dinner–flour fish and seasonings.

7. They wanted us–Alice and me–to meet them at the park.

8. I took Callie–my calico cat–to the vet.

9. Frank asked Bill to bring three things to the party–music soda and chips.

10. Let's go to the park–oh wait, we promised to meet Mary at the movie.

Choose your **STRENGTH** exercise!

Exercise for today:

Day 7

Check & Record in Fitness Log.

Do you have a place where you and your friends gather to meet? Maybe a favorite mall or park? The ancient Romans had a place to gather – the Forum. It was located in the valley between two of the seven hills where Rome was built.

The Forum was the main business center and shopping area for the Romans. They would do banking, trading and shopping. It was also a place for speeches. Government officials, religious leaders, or anyone who wanted to speak out was able to speak. In fact, good oration (public speaking) was considered a gift. The orator's purpose was to convince, to share ideas, but not to argue. People would stop their shopping or their visiting and listen to the speaker.

The Forum was also a place for religious ceremonies. There were temples to some of the gods that the people worshiped, so a shopper might stop and offer a gift to a god on their way home.

Festivals were also celebrated in the Forum. They might have to do with the seasons, a military conquest, or weddings.

Circle the things you would not find at the forum.

chariot	temple	sheep	car	benches
shops	mannequin	statues	food	
radio	aqueduct	mailbox	children	public speakers

Review Divide by 1 digit

1. $9 \overline{)891}$ $\frac{99}{}$

2. $6 \overline{)822}$ 137

3. $4 \overline{)996}$ 249

4. $6 \overline{)547}$ $91\frac{1}{6}$

5. $499 \div 9 = 55\,4/9$

6. $905 \div 6 = 150\,5/6$

$55\,4/9$
$9\overline{)499}$

$150\frac{5}{6}$
$6\overline{)905}$

6-7 • © Summer Fit Activities™

Circle the number of each sentence that uses commas, parentheses and dashes correctly.

1. Several of my friends – Joanne, Marlene, Eve and Joan – are going to the party.
2. I am going to tell you a great story – but, the movie is ready to start.
3. Joe who is, my best friend, is meeting me at the mall.
4. I think the moose the cat and the cougar are very interesting animals.
5. Our class president (would you believe it) forgot to vote in the election.
6. Pennies, nickels, dimes, and quarters – these are the coins most often used.
7. She is going to Hawaii (a place) she always wanted to see.
8. Francis (who had brought his computer with him) googled the answer to the questions.
9. Most of the guests were eating (except for Ann who wasn't feeling well).
10. The price ($65) of the (shoes) seemed outrageous.
11. I just got a haircut – and it looks terrible!
12. Frank found pickles, onions, and tomato on his sandwich – which he loved.
13. The boys talked about cars movies and, music.
14. My friend – Sam – went with me to the movie today.
15. The teacher, Mrs. Brand, helped the students plan the car wash.

Divide 4 digits with decimal by 1 digit.

Remember that when the only decimal is in the dividend, the decimal in your answer needs to line up with the decimal in the dividend.

1. $9 \overline{) 1.089}$ → .121

2. $8 \overline{) 200.8}$ → 25.1

3. $7 \overline{) 394.1}$ → 563

4. $332.4 \div 4 =$ 83.1

$4 \overline{) 332.4}$ → 83.1

5. $31.38 \div 6 =$ 5.23

$6 \overline{) 31.38}$ → 5.23

Choose your AEROBIC exercise!

Exercise for today:

Check & Record in Fitness Log.

Day 8

Hyperbole (pronounced hi-per-bo-lee) is another word for exaggeration. We have talked about how hyperbole is an element of tall tales. People use hyperbole in everyday speech as well, and it is sometimes found in other genres of literature. Below are some commonly used examples of hyperbole. Write what each one means (without using exaggeration.)

1. I am so hungry I could eat a horse. *I am very hungry.*
2. I have a million things to do. *I have lots of errens to run.*
3. I had a ton of homework. *I have lots of homework to do.*
4. If I can't buy that new dress, I will die. *I really want to buy that new dress.*
5. He is as skinny as a toothpick. *He is very skinny.*
6. This car goes faster than the speed of light. *The car goes really fast.*
7. That new car costs a bazillion dollars. *The new car cost a lot of money.*
8. That joke is so old, the last time I heard it I was riding on a dinosaur. *That joke is really old.*
9. He's got tons of money. *He has lots of money.*
10. You could have knocked me over with a feather. *You could knock me over easily.*
11. I've told you a million times. *I have told you a lot of times.*
12. He is older than the hills. *He is very old.*

Convection

Heat energy transferred by the movement of a liquid or gas is called convection. When particles are heated, they move faster, expand, become less dense, and 'bang,' the particles rise. As the liquid or gas cools, the particles move slower, contract, become more dense, and 'bang,' the particles sink. This movement of heating, expanding, rising, cooling, contracting, and sinking is a continuous one. An example is to observe the amount of wind in the early morning compared to the afternoon. Wind is an example of a convection process in motion.

For this activity you need food coloring, distilled water, salt, a freezer tray for ice cubes, and two glass jars. Mix some of the distilled water with a few drops of food coloring. Freeze this into cubes. Fill two glass jars 3/4 full with distilled water. Add some salt to one of the jars and label it. Place a colored cube in each jar of water. Observe the movement of the colored water as it melts into the warmer water. Do not move the jars. Can you identify convection currents? Where is the colored water going? Is the colored cold water heavier or lighter than the warmer clear water?

Write three sentences telling your observations and conclusions.

I learned that when particles are heated they move faster. They also expand, and become less dense and 'bangs' the partilcals. Also Wind is a convection process in motion.

Affixes are syllables or words attached to the beginnings (prefixes) or the ends (suffixes) of root words. A root word is the basic word, from which deeper meaning can be gained by adding prefixes and suffixes. Here are some common affixes and their meanings.

Anti – against or opposite   Pre - before

In – not   Pro – for

Ir – not   Sub - under

Mis – wrong   Super - above

Post – after   Trans – across

Use these meaning, and what you know of the meanings of the root words to define the following:

1. pro – British _____

2. inhuman *not human* _____

3. substandard *under standard* _____

4. misspell *wrong spell* _____

5. anti-inflammatory *against inflammatory* _____

6. superhuman *above human* _____

7. irregular *not regular* _____

8. transatlantic *across atlantic* _____

9. incorrect *not correct* _____

10. postscript *after script* _____

Choose your STRENGTH exercise!

Exercise for today:

_____

Check & Record in Fitness Log.

Day 9

Compassion - Oprah Winfrey

Oprah Winfrey survived a childhood of abuse and neglect. She has become a well-known individual of influence and success. She uses her success and influence to reach out to others.

Oprah campaigned for a national database of convicted child abusers. She testified before a U.S. Senate Judiciary Committee on behalf of a National Child Protection Act. The "Oprah Bill," which established that database, became a law in 1993, and is available to law enforcement agencies around the country.

Oprah believes in using your life to help others. In 2000, Oprah's Angel Network began presenting a $100,000 "Use Your Life Award" to people who are using their own lives to improve the lives of others. She promotes other philanthropic ventures as well. One organization she has helped is the Oprah Winfrey Leadership Academy for Girls, near Johannesburg, South Africa. She initiated *Christmas Kindness South Africa*, which allowed 50,000 children from orphanages and rural schools in South Africa to receive food, clothing, and school supplies.

1. What is a definition of the word neglect? _When somebody fails to care for you proporly_

2. What is a definition of the word influence? _persuade or convince somebody._

3. In what country is Oprah's Leadership Academy for Girls? _Johannesburg, South Africa_

4. After reading Oprah's story, how would you explain the value of compassion? Give an example of someone you know who demonstrates compassion.

   I am commpasion of me doing without my partents telling me to, so they do not get annoyed

Value: COMPASSION

Having compassion means showing kindness, caring and a willingness to help others who may be sick, hurt, poor, or in need. When you have compassion you are putting yourself in someone else's shoes and really feeling for them. You can do this in very small ways for example when your friend trips and falls. You can do this in larger ways when someone you know does not have enough food to eat.

> "Love and compassion are necessities not luxuries. Without them, humanity cannot survive."
> – Dalai Lama

Unscramble the letters to reveal the traits of being a Hero of Compassion.

dnik _kind_

ufltuhgtoh _thoughtful_

aricgn _caring_

udantnesinrgd _understanding_

epilngh _helping_

ielgnsnti _listening_

rstceandoei _considerate_

ronfmoicgt _comforting_

avber _brave_

tpaenti _patient_

Make a "Compassion Jar". Cut out several slips of paper and write on each a way to show compassion. For example: Hold the door for someone, smile at a stranger, or read to a younger child. Choose one to do each day.

(kind) (thoughtful) (caring) (understanding) (helping)
(listening) (considerate) (comforting) (brave) (patient)

Choose a Play or Exercise Activity!

INCENTIVE CONTRACT CALENDAR

My parents and I agree that if I complete this section of

Summer Fit Activities™

and read _____ minutes a day, my reward will be _____

Child Signature: _____ Parent Signature: _____

Day 1			Day 6		
Day 2			Day 7		
Day 3			Day 8		
Day 4			Day 9		
Day 5			Day 10		

Color the for each day of activities completed.

Color the for each day of reading completed.

Summer Fitness Log

Choose your exercise activity each day from the Aerobic and Strength Activities in the back of the book. Record the date, stretch, activity and how long you performed your exercise activity below. Fill in how many days you complete your fitness activity on your Incentive Contract Calendars.

	Date	Stretch	Activity	Time
examples:	June 4	Run in place	Sky Reach	7 min
	June 5	Toe Touches	Bottle Curls	15 min
1.				
2.				
3.				
4.				
5.				
6.				
7.				
8.				
9.				
10.				

I promise to do my best for me. I exercise to be healthy and active. I am awesome because I am me.

Child Signature: _____

6-7 • © Summer Fit Activities™

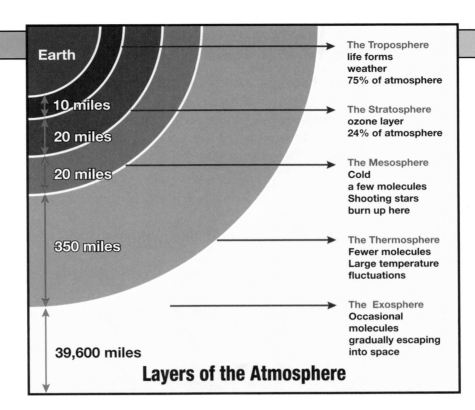

Layers of the Atmosphere

Use the diagram to help you match each layer of the atmosphere with its description.

1. The layer that we live in, made out of the gases we breathe every day, is called the

   The Troposphere

2. The layer which blends into the thermosphere, in which molecules may escape into space, is the

   The Exosphere

3. The ozone layer, which makes up about 24% of the atmosphere is

   The Stratosphere

4. The layer with large temperature fluctuations and fewer molecules is

   The Thermosphere

5. This layer is cold, with few molecules. Shooting stars burn up here

   The Mesosphere

Divide numbers with decimal by 2 digits with decimal.

Now, you have to think. The decimal in the divisor means you need to move the decimal one place to the right and move the decimal in the dividend one place to the right. Then place the decimal in the answer immediately above the one in the dividend.

1. $2.6 \overline{)738.4}$

2. $7.1 \overline{)163.33}$

3. $63 \overline{)114.03}$

4. $434.2 \div 5.2 =$

5. $348.08 \div 3.8 =$

Figurative language is important to literature. Its usage provides depth, clarity, and interest to a selection. Some examples are idiom, metaphor, simile, hyperbole, and personification. Authors also use puns and irony. Figurative language can also be words put together in such a way as to catch the reader's interest because of the sound created, such as alliteration, assonance, rhyme or onomatopoeia. Here are some definitions and examples of commonly used figures of speech.

Idiom - words that have meaning different from their literal meaning – She was pulling his leg.

Metaphor – a direct comparison of two unlike things that have a specific thing in common – Life is a journey.

Simile – a direct comparison using the words "like" or "as" – Life is like a journey.

Hyperbole – exaggeration – He is a hundred feet tall.

Personification – giving human qualities to a nonhuman thing – The stars danced playfully in the sky.

Pun – a saying where one word or phrase has two meanings, a literal one and a funny one – Old owls never die; they just don't give a hoot.

Irony – A statement in which there is a discordance beyond the evident meaning - You study all week for a spelling test, then misspell your name.

Alliteration – repetition of the same beginning sound – The boy bounced the ball boisterously.

Assonance – repetition of a vowel sound – He rode on a proud round cloud.

Rhyme – having the same ending sound, at the end of lines of poetry or within a phrase – I had a fright in the bright night

Onomatopoeia – a word that imitates a sound associated with that word – Bam, bang, clank went the car.

Now it's your turn to have some fun. Write at three sentences using some of these types of figurative language.

1. I scream for ice cream!

2. that is so punny!

3. He is like a skunk, always so dirty!

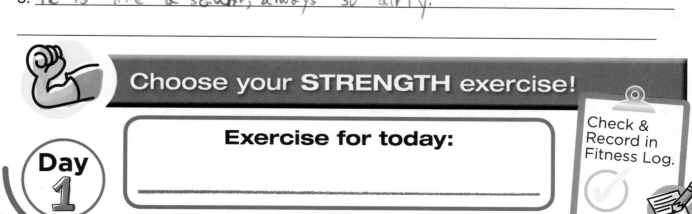

Choose your **STRENGTH** exercise!

Day 1

Exercise for today:

Check & Record in Fitness Log.

Greatest Common Factor

When one number is divisible by a second, the second number is called a factor of the first. Two numbers may have some factors that are the same. These numbers are called common factors. The greatest of the common factors of two numbers is called their greatest common factor (GCF). An easy way to find the factors is to make a T chart. You begin with the smallest factor and the factor it needs to multiply to get the number. Then use the next factor, etc.

Example   36

1	36
2	18
3	(12)
4	9
6	6

Notice that 5 is not a factor of 36, so it is not on the chart. When the next number you could use is already on the right side, you have all the factors. Try using the T chart on the right to factor the number 48.

48

1	48
2	24
3	16
4	(12)
6	8

Now that you have the factors of both numbers, put a circle around the numbers that are in both charts (common.) Then decide which of the circled numbers is largest – that is the GCF. Remember that the GCF may be one of the numbers you are factoring.

On a separate sheet of paper, use T charts to find the GCF of these pairs of numbers:

1. 5 and 15 _____   2. 12 and 24 _____   3. 18 and 21 _____   4. 15 and 18 _____

In writing, argument does not involve anger. It involves using reason and logic to make a point. You are trying to persuade someone of your position, but you are not emotionally involved in the argument. During the summer, many people take a vacation. Parents don't go to work, children don't go to school. Sometimes people stay home but do a variety of activities available in their area. Other people decide to go somewhere else – either a favorite spot or a brand new place. Your task is to write a paragraph stating which you think is the better vacation (stay home or go somewhere) and why. You need at least three well-stated reasons. Use a separate sheet of paper if needed.

I think staying home for a vaction is a great idea. One reason I think this is because if you go to some other place and don't like it, you are stuck there. Another reason is you can play with your friends at home and laze around to. My last reason is because staying home saves money. Usally, when you go on vacation you spend more money, than if you were at home. And that is why I would like to stay at home insted of going on a vacation!

Around the year 1200, the kingdom of Ghana, in Africa, fell apart. The kingdom of Mali took over. The new king was a young man named Sundiata. He knew that trade was critical to Mali's success as a country, so he worked to restore trade alliances with Mali's neighbors. Mali grew in size under Sundiata's leadership. There were gold mines in the south and salt mines in the north. These both became very precious trade commodities.

Sundiata was a hero to his people. He was nicknamed the Lion King. Besides improving trade, he also built a strong military, to protect his country and the trade routes. He was a Muslim, but he believed in religious freedom. Unlike many kings of his time, when he conquered a new place, he did not make people convert to his religion, but allowed them to keep their own. He also allowed slaves to work for their freedom. He ruled for 25 years, and his people loved him.

1. Why would the nickname Lion King be an appropriate nickname for Sundiata? _____
Lions were undefetoble back then, and a Lion king would mean great power and thing like that.

2. Of the things Sundiata did to improve Mali, which do you think is most important? Why?
He worked to restore trade alliances with Mali's neighbors, so Mali could become a more succesful contrey.

Multiple Meanings

Many words have more than one definition. It is a task of the reader to find the best meaning for the way the word is used in a sentence. **The nonsense sentences below confuse two meanings of the underlined words. Briefly tell what the two meanings are.**

1. The computer mouse ate the cheese. _① The animal mouse. ② a computer mouse to control your curser on your computer_

2. Hailey will take a trip next week on a banana peel. _① a vaction trip. ② when you slip._

3. Spring is my favorite season and cinnamon is not. _① Spring is a season. ② cinnamon is a kind of topping/food_

4. Everyone was present today, including the gift. _① being there. ② a gift._

5. In a second, he would win the medal between first and third. _① a time unit. ② a rank._

Choose your AEROBIC exercise!

Exercise for today:

Day 2

Check & Record in Fitness Log.

GCF

Use GCF to rewrite expression such as $36 + 8 = 4(9+2)$. Find the GCF of the two numbers. Divide the two numbers by the GCF to find the factors that belong in the parenthesis.

1. $42 - 14 = 7(6-2)$
2. $36 - 18 = 18(2-1)$
3. $12 + 36 = 12(1+3)$
4. $15 + 18 = 3(5+6)$
5. $21 - 18 = 3(7-6)$
6. $44 - 12 = 4(11-3)$

7. $42 - 12 = 3(14-4)$
8. $21 + 18 = 3(7+6)$
9. $36 - 24 = 12(3-2)$
10. $45 - 30 = 5(9-6)$
11. $21 + 42 = 7(3+6)$
12. $36 - 27 = 9(4-3)$

Aesop's Fables

The legend is that a Greek man named Aesop was an ancient creator of many wonderful fables (a fable is a story which teaches a lesson or a moral). Tradition says that he was a slave who was able to earn his freedom because his master so enjoyed his stories. Many stories have been attributed to Aesop. There are also fables in many other cultures. One favorite fable attributed to Aesop is *The Lion and the Mouse*.

The lion was proud and strong, and king of the jungle. One day while he was sleeping, a tiny mouse ran over his face. The great lion awoke with a snarl. He caught the mouse with one mighty paw and raised the other to squash the creature who had annoyed him.

"Oh please, mighty lion!" squeaked the mouse, please do not kill me. Let me go, I beg you. If you do, one day I may be able to help in some way."

This greatly amused the lion. The thought that such a small and frightened creature as a mouse might be able to help the king of the jungle was so funny that he did not have the heart to kill the mouse. "Go away" he growled.

A few days later, a party of hunters came into the jungle. They decided to try to capture the lion. They climbed two trees, one on each side of the path, and held a net over the path. Later in the day the lion came loping along the path. At once the hunters dropped their net on the great beast. The lion roared and fought mightily, but he could not escape from the net.

The hunters went off to eat, leaving the lion trapped in the net, unable to move. The lion roared for help, but the only creature in the jungle that dared come near was the tiny mouse.

"Oh, it's you," groaned the lion. "There's nothing you can do to help me. You're too small."

"I may be small," said the mouse, "but I have sharp teeth and I owe you a good turn!"

Then the mouse began to nibble at the net. Before long he had made a hole big enough to allow the lion to crawl through and make his escape into the jungle.

MORAL: Sometimes the weak are able to help the strong.

1. Why did the lion let the mouse go free? _The lion did not have the heart to kill the mouse._

2. How was the mouse able to help the lion? _He nibble a big hole through the net, leading the lion to escape_

3. Why were the hunters not worried about leaving the lion? _They were not worried because the lion would not come back for them or eat them._

4. Give another example of the weak helping the strong. _When your big friend is sad of something, you can make him feel better._

6-7 • © Summer Fit Activities™

A synonym is a word that means the same or about the same thing as another word. Use of synonyms can help your writing become more interesting as it clarifies meaning and helps you to not be repetitive.

Read this myth about the White goddess of the moon, then find synonyms for the words listed below.

Artemis was the twin sister of the god of the sun, Apollo. She was ambitious, ruthless and hard-hearted. She was not gentle, like her mother Leto. She had a mind like a steel trap. When she wanted something, she went for it.

Artemis was resentful that Apollo had more of the world than she had. It wasn't fair! When Apollo came home the night after his first ride with the Horses of the Sun, Artemis was quite proud of him. But she said, "Look, brother," you've traveled all over – to the Hyperboreans and everywhere – all those beautiful places. You traveled in that fancy chariot with the swans and the dolphins. Now our father, Zeus, gives you the Horses of the Sun and nothing for me! It's not fair!" She went on to say that the next morning she would go with him to Mount Olympus. She would remind her father that she was his daughter, the Sun God's twin. If Apollo had the chariot of Helius to light up the day, she must have the silvery fire of Selene to light the sky at night. (Selene drove a silver chariot with two white horses over the night sky.)

Quite early the next morning the brother and sister rose up to Olympus. Zeus had not expected to see his lovely daughter; it had been a long time since she had visited. But when he saw her, this White Goddess, chaste and fair, he saw the logic of her request. What the brother could do in the day, the sister could do in the night. So he made the White Goddess the keeper of the silvery moon.

1. Find a synonym for the word pure.

2. Find a synonym for the word bitter.

3. Find a synonym for the word carriage.

4. Find a synonym for the word remorseless.

5. Find a synonym for the word anticipate.

Choose your STRENGTH exercise!

Exercise for today:

Check & Record in Fitness Log.

Day 3

6–7 • © Summer Fit Activities™

Least Common Multiple

The first step in finding the LCM is to list 5 multiples of each number (knowing that the number itself is also a multiple.) So the next 5 multiples of 2 are 4, 6, 8, 10, 12. After you list the multiples of two numbers, you look for the smallest one that is the same in each list.

List the next 5 multiples of each number below.

1. 3, ___, ___, ___, ___, ___

2. 4, ___, ___, ___, ___, ___

3. 5, ___, ___, ___, ___, ___

4. 6, ___, ___, ___, ___, ___

5. 7, ___, ___, ___, ___, ___

6. 8, ___, ___, ___, ___, ___

7. 9, ___, ___, ___, ___, ___

Now, find the LCM of these sets of numbers.

8. 2 and 5 _____   9. 6 and 8 _____   10. 2, 3 and 5 _____   11. 3, 6 and 9 _____

Location

There are five themes in the study of geography: Location, place, movement, human environment interaction, and region (a good mnemonic device for remembering these is **Little Purple Men Hop Everywhere In Rome**).

Location can be exact or relative. An example of an exact location is your address. Map coordinates are another example of exact location. Relative location means where something is located in relation to something else. The Statue of Liberty is in a harbor by New York City.

The locations of ancient civilizations had a lot to do with what resources were available. People tended to settle near areas that had good land for farming, fairly level land for building homes, and rivers. Rivers were one of the most important resources people could find. The civilizations we have studied so far – Mesopotamia, Egypt, Greece, Rome, China, and Mali – were all located near major rivers.

Rivers served many purposes. Sometimes they were a barrier which prevented other groups of people from attacking and conquering, but people also did everyday sorts of things in rivers: they collected water for drinking and cooking, they used it for washing, they fished, they traveled to trade with other groups, and even took leisurely boat rides.

In India, civilization grew up near the Indus River Valley. We don't know as much about this society as some of the others we've studied, but in 1922, archaeologists uncovered the ancient cities of Harappa and Mohenjo-Daro. We know that the women wore lipstick, children had whistles and other toys, and artisans made beautiful pottery.

1. Give the absolute location of your home (your address) _____

2. Give a relative location of your home (what it is near) _____

3. List three reasons rivers were important to early civilizations _____

_____

_____

Antonyms are words that are opposites of another word. It's useful to recognize common antonyms. **In the exercise below, match the pairs of antonyms in each set**.

1. _____ abandon
2. _____ distinct
3. _____ delight
4. _____ loosen
5. _____ anxious

a. agony
b. tighten
c. keep
d. unconcerned
e. indistinguishable

6. _____ squander
7. _____ dilemma
8. _____ scanty
9. _____ partial
10. _____ plain

a. solution
b. complete
c. economize
d. ample
e. lavish

11. _____ failure
12. _____ accurate
13. _____ permit
14. _____ often
15. _____ fluid

a. mistaken
b. success
c. solid
d. forbid
e. rarely

Equivalent fractions

Fractions that name the same number are called equivalent fractions. A set of equivalent fractions might be 1/2 ≈ 2/4 ≈ 5/10. Equivalent fractions are written by multiplying or dividing both the numerator and the denominator by the same number.

Examples:

$$\frac{1}{2} = \frac{1 \times 3}{2 \times 3} = \frac{3}{6}$$

$$\frac{10}{45} = \frac{10 \div 5}{45 \div 5} = \frac{2}{9}$$

1. $\dfrac{3}{9} = \dfrac{3 \div 3}{9 \div 3} =$

2. $\dfrac{1}{2} = \dfrac{7}{14}$

3. $\dfrac{1}{5} = \dfrac{5}{25}$

4. $\dfrac{8}{72} = \dfrac{1}{9}$

Choose your AEROBIC exercise!

Exercise for today:

Day 4

Check & Record in Fitness Log.

Trustworthiness - Walter Cronkite

Value

Do you trust what you see on TV or hear on the radio? A good dose of skepticism is often wise, Walter Cronkite was a newsman who was called the most trusted man in America.

Cronkite covered stories from World War II through the Vietnam conflict. He knew Presidents Truman, Eisenhower, Nixon, Kennedy, Johnson, and Reagan. He researched his information carefully, and was careful in his presentation of his stories. He said his job was to report the information, not to be a commentator or an analyst. Because he kept to the facts, and the facts were correct, the American public trusted him. If Walter Cronkite said something, it must be true.

Cronkite received many awards throughout his journalistic career, for his contributions to journalism. He was awarded the Presidential Medal of Freedom by President Jimmy Carter. From Princeton University, he was awarded the James Madison Award for Distinguished Public Service. His contributions to the broadcast business gave the American people someone they could trust.

1. Name 4 of the presidents Cronkite knew.

   Kennedy , Johnson ,

   Truman , Nixon .

2. Define skepticism: Skepticism means to lie about something.

3. Why did the American public trust Walter Cronkite? Give at least 2 reasons. He kept to the facts, and the facts were correct, and he reasearched information carefully.

4. Which president awarded Cronkite the Presidential Medal of Freedom? President Jimmy Carter.

Value: TRUSTWORTHINESS

FAMILY ACTIVITIES

Choose one or more activities to do with your family or friends.

 Talk about ways you show you are trustworthy. Remember that when you are dishonest and not truthful, people will not trust you. Think about the times you have been trustworthy. Write down at least 5 words that describe how you felt being trusted.

 Talk about what it means to be a trustworthy friend. Make a Friendship bracelet and give it to one of your friends. Let them know they can count on you to be a good friend.

 Write down the word TRUSTWORTHY. How many little words can you make from the letters?

VALUES ARE A FAMILY AFFAIR

Read more about TRUSTWORTHINESS

Wish You Well
By David Baldacci

The Cay
By Theodore Taylor

To Kill A Mockingbird
By Harper Lee

Choose a game or activity to play for 60 minutes as a family or with friends today!

Day 5
Choose a Play or Exercise Activity!

Summer Explorer

Healthy Planet Activities and Fun Things to Do!

- Have a book exchange with your friends.

- Make your own musical instruments out of cardboard boxes and perform a song.

- Create a healthy dinner menu for your family.

- Visit a lake, river, or pond. Bring a notebook to do some nature drawings.

- Make your own bubble solution. Go outside and make some enormous bubbles.

- Pick wildflowers and arrange them in a glass or jar.

- Draw a flipbook.

- Make cookies for a neighbor — deliver them with someone.

- Go to the park with a friend.

- Sign up for a free project at Home Depot, Lowes, or Michaels.

- Make a scavenger hunt to do with friends or family.

- Plant something: flowers, vegetables, herbs, a tree.

- Read to a younger child.

- Make a photo album or scrapbook.

- Try a new cookie recipe.

- Have a water balloon fight.

- Help an elderly neighbor weed his/her garden.

- Paint or draw a self-portrait.

Giant Bubbles

6 cups Water
1/2 cup Dish Soap (Dawn blue)
1/2 cup Cornstarch
1 TBSP Baking Powder
1 TBSP Glycerin
(Glycerin found in cake decoration aisle at craft store)

1 Slowly mix together in large bucket or dishpan.

2 Let solution sit for 1-2 hours.

3 Tie a length of string between two straws to make a bubble wand or use store bought wands. The bigger your wand, the bigger your bubbles!

6–7 • © Summer Fit Activities™

Summer Journal II

Write about your family vacation.

6-7 • © Summer Fit Activities™

Cross products

Cross products are a simple way to check if two fractions are equivalent.

Example: $\frac{2}{9}$ $\frac{4}{18}$ 2 x 18 = 36   4 x 9 = 36   If the two crossed products equal the same thing, the fractions are equivalent.

Check the cross products to determine if the pairs of fractions are equivalent. Circle those that are.

1. $\frac{3}{9}$ $\frac{9}{15}$

2. $\frac{2}{5}$ $\frac{6}{10}$

3. $\frac{1}{5}$ $\frac{4}{16}$

4. $\frac{5}{5}$ $\frac{9}{9}$

5. $\frac{8}{12}$ $\frac{9}{13}$

6. $\frac{3}{8}$ $\frac{6}{16}$

7. $\frac{8}{12}$ $\frac{12}{18}$

Olmec

The first civilization we know of in Middle America (also called Mesoamerica) is the Olmec. These people built huge stone images of their rulers and their gods. Many were taller than a man, and weighed over 40 tons. Some of these were transported great distances, and to our knowledge they did not use wheels or animals. Makes you wonder how they managed it!

Look at the picture of the giant stone head. What does it tell you about the Olmec people? Did they think this god or ruler was kind or tyrannical? Was he intelligent or foolish? Was he handsome or ordinary?

If you were responsible for depicting the god of the Olmec people, how would you draw him? What facial features would you use? What designs or decorations would you incorporate?

Draw your version below.

Spelling

Spelling is an important skill in communication. Below are several groups of words.
Circle the one in each group which is spelled correctly.

1.	lenth	amoung	station	polece
2.	lying	saylor	reapeats	picher
3.	distanse	curtain	anser	carefull
4.	plesure	propper	butcher	persanal
5.	freinds	daughter	engin	somtimes
6.	degrea	terible	dutey	surprise
7.	companey	complaint	reletive	measur
8.	passengers	twelfe	entranse	importanse
9.	ninteen	hungrey	knowen	lining
10.	remaned	nepheew	whisper	langwage
11.	liberary	rhythm	ridiculus	legitemate
12.	divine	knowlidge	assinement	budjet
13.	condem	sciance	mathmatics	fulfill
14.	permenent	asterick	kindergarten	analize
15.	irelevent	admisable	attendance	canidate

Compare fractions

Write < or > to compare each set of fractions.

Example: $\dfrac{3}{5} > \dfrac{4}{7}$ $\dfrac{3}{5} = \dfrac{21}{35}$ $\dfrac{4}{7} = \dfrac{20}{35}$ Compare the new fractions $\dfrac{21}{35} > \dfrac{20}{35}$ so $\dfrac{3}{5} > \dfrac{4}{7}$

1. $\dfrac{5}{9}$ $\dfrac{4}{15}$	2. $\dfrac{4}{5}$ $\dfrac{7}{10}$	3. $\dfrac{3}{5}$ $\dfrac{3}{16}$	4. $\dfrac{7}{5}$ $\dfrac{3}{9}$	5. $\dfrac{5}{8}$ $\dfrac{3}{4}$	6. $\dfrac{1}{2}$ $\dfrac{3}{8}$

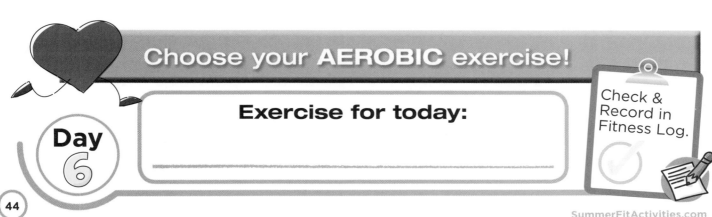

Choose your AEROBIC exercise!

Exercise for today:

Check & Record in Fitness Log.

Day 6

6-7 • © Summer Fit Activities™

Rhyme Scheme

Remember that the rhyme scheme is the pattern formed by the rhyming words in a poem. Use letters to designate the lines that rhyme with each other. **For each of the poem segments below, write the rhyme scheme.**

Example: Fiddle-dee-dee by Eugene Field

There once was a bird that lived up in a tree,
And all he could whistle was "Fiddle-dee-dee" -
A very provoking, unmusical song
For one to be whistling the summer day long!
Yet always contented and busy was he
With that vocal recurrence of "Fiddle-dee-dee."   Rhyme Scheme: AABBCC

1.   An Astrologer's Song by Rudyard Kipling

To the Heavens above us
O look and behold
The Planets that love us
All harnessed in gold!
What chariots, what horses
Against us shall bide
While the Stars in their courses
Do fight on our side?

Rhyme Scheme : _____

2.   Children by Henry Wadsworth Longfellow

Come to me, O ye children!
For I hear you at your play,
And the questions that perplexed me
Have vanished quite away.

Rhyme Scheme : _____

3.   A Little Bird I Am by Louisa May Alcott

A little bird I am,
Shut from the fields of air,
And in my cage I sit and sing
To Him who placed me there:
Well pleased a prisoner to be,
Because, my God, it pleases Thee!
Naught have I else to do;
I sing the whole day long;
And He whom most I love to please
Doth listen to my song,
He caught and bound my wandering wing,
But still He bends to hear me sing.

Rhyme Scheme : _____

Sentence fragments

Many people get in a hurry when they are writing. Sometimes this causes people to write incomplete sentences. There are times when an author does this on purpose. To make a point, right? (That was an example.) However, very often it is not on purpose and it is confusing to the reader.

Mark each of the following sentences as **C** for complete or **I** for incomplete.

1. _____ Few rainy days in May.
2. _____ Luke always seems to be living in his own world.
3. _____ Even when it is full of music, food, and games.
4. _____ One very happy person in Silver City.
5. _____ Because it is quick and easy.
6. _____ She changes her plans if it is raining.
7. _____ The books on the table were overdue at the library.
8. _____ Sometimes it pays to look up.
9. _____ When I first saw this path.
10. _____ Toys of all kinds thrown everywhere.
11. _____ Mr. Jones gone to the market for groceries.
12. _____ Driving in the city in the early morning.
13. _____ When my cousin moved to New York, he had a hard time making new friends.
14. _____ Suzanne loved to go shopping with her mother and her aunts.

Phases of the Moon
Match the phase names with the description
New Moon
Waxing Crescent
Waxing Gibbous
Full Moon
Waning Gibbous
Waning Crescent

First Quarter
Waxing Gibbous Waxing Crescent

Full   **View From Earth**   New

Waning Gibbous   Waning Crescent
Third Quarter

1. This moon occurs when the moon is on the opposite
   side of the earth; presents a full round disc. _____

2. The first of the moon phases (very little of the moon is showing). _____

3. Waxing means growing, and this moon is in the shape of a crescent. _____

4. A Gibbous moon is bulging out; this moon is still growing. _____

5. Waning is shrinking; this moon is again in the shape of a crescent. _____

6. This moon is shrinking and bulging at the same time. _____

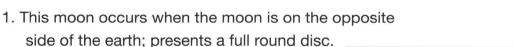

Choose your STRENGTH exercise!

Exercise for today:

Day 7

Check & Record in Fitness Log.

Aztec

When the Aztecs arrived in central Mexico, they found the best land already occupied by other groups. Normally when the Aztec came to a new place they would fight with the current occupants and take over the land. However this time, there was a legend involved. The legend said that when they spotted an eagle, perched on a cactus, holding a snake, they were to settle down. They were to live peacefully with their neighbors until they had gained strength. Finally, they were to build a glorious Aztec city, a city of their own.

They settled on the swampy land next to Lake Texcoco, where they began to build the most fantastic thing – floating gardens! This is an example of Human Environment Interaction. There wasn't the best land for farming in the swamps they initially inhabited. They built their own farmland by building rafts and anchoring them to the lakebed. They piled reeds and other vegetation on top of the rafts, and dirt on top of that. They used these gardens to grow chili peppers, squash, tomatoes, beans, and corn.

The Aztecs created more land by filling in the swamps and marshland. They built a glorious city in the middle of Lake Texcoco, named Tenochtitlan. The city had huge temples, open plazas, and a busy marketplace. There were "eating houses" and hairdressers.

The current capital of Mexico, Mexico City, is built on this same site. The lake is covered up except for a few small pockets of water and some underground waterways. The Aztec left a lasting reminder of their civilization.

1. Explain how the humans interacted with their environment in Tenochtitlan. _____

_____

2. What can you infer from the fact that the current capital of Mexico is on the same site as the

Aztec capital of Tenochtitlan? _____

3. What did the Aztec do with their city or their gardens that was a surprise to you? _____

_____

Simile

A simile is a comparison between two unlike things that have something in common. It uses the words "like" or "as" to signify the comparison. In the description "shoots up taller like an india-rubber ball," the implication is that a rubber ball bounces very high, very suddenly and that sometimes the shadow becomes very tall, very suddenly.

What do each of these similes mean?

1. as alike as two peas in a pod _____

2. as big as a bus _____

3. as black as coal _____

4. as blind as a bat _____

In the following sentences, circle the two things being compared in each.

5. The sink was as clean as a whistle.

6. As Mark stood outside in the snow, he began to feel as cold as ice.

7. Claire was very tricky, causing her friends to think she was as clever as a fox.

8. After winning the science fair competition, Pierre was as proud as a peacock.

Some compound words use a hyphen – some do not. Some examples are: eyewitness, eye shadow, eye-opener. You have to just know them or look them up in a dictionary. If you can't find it in the dictionary, assume they are two separate words.

Hyphenate a pair of adjectives when they come before a noun and act as a single idea. She is a friendly-looking woman. (If you could use "and" between the adjectives, do not hyphenate.)

When adverbs not ending in –ly are used as compound words in front of a noun, hyphenate. When they come after noun, do not hyphenate. He got some much-needed sleep. He got some sleep which was much needed.

Hyphenate numbers from twenty-one through ninety-nine, and all spelled out fractions.

Hyphens are also used to separate a word into syllables when the word has to be broken.

Circle the numbers of the sentences that are hyphenated correctly.

1. Marty needed a full-time job to pay for the books he needed for his classes.
2. Samantha had a sweet-sunny disposition.
3. The team needed six-teen points to win the game.
4. There were twenty-seven cans of peaches in the pantry.
5. I counted sixty-six cars on the train as it went by.
6. The restaurant boasted an award-winning hamburger.
7. We went to fif-teen houses trying to sell Girl Scout cookies.
8. They made a movie with a very low-budget.
9. The well-trained dog took first place in the championship contest.
10. The group used a specific decision-making process to arrive at a solution.

Simplify fractions

For most problems involving fractions, you will be asked to put the answer in its lowest term or simplify. To simplify a fraction, you divide the numerator and the denominator by the same number. You can divide both by the GCF.

1. $\dfrac{26}{39} \div \dfrac{13}{13}$ 2. $\dfrac{8}{24}$ 3. $\dfrac{12}{36}$ 4. $\dfrac{16}{40}$ 5. $\dfrac{7}{28}$

6. $\dfrac{14}{28}$ 7. $\dfrac{8}{40}$ 8. $\dfrac{24}{36}$ 9. $\dfrac{15}{24}$ 10. $\dfrac{9}{36}$

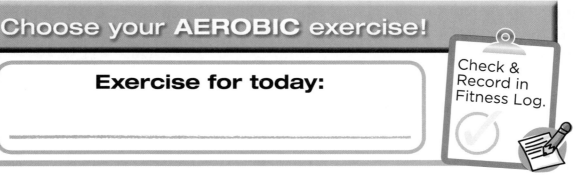

Choose your AEROBIC exercise!

Exercise for today:

Check & Record in Fitness Log.

Day 8

How constellations move

Have you noticed that constellations seem to move across the sky? This is because the earth rotates on its axis. The earth rotates from west to east. The stars maintain their position in the sky. We say a constellation has risen in the sky, but really the earth has rotated so that we can see particular constellations.

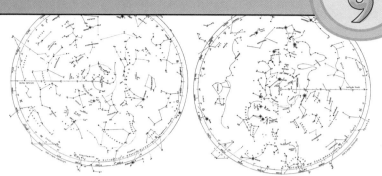

In addition, the earth moves around the sun once a year. The zodiac constellations are visible at different points in that orbit. For example, Orion is visible during the northern winter, but is on the opposite side of the sun during the summer, and therefore is not visible.

Try this experiment. Go out one night when the Moon is visible and try to find some stars that appear close to the Moon. You might want to draw a picture showing the Moon and the location of these stars. Try to go out the next night at the same time and compare your drawing to what you see. The stars you drew should be in about the same spot as the night before but the Moon will have moved. What happened? The stars are in the same spot because the Earth spun around once. The reason why the Moon isn't quite where you saw it the night before is because the Moon is orbiting the Earth.

1. Which moves, the earth or the constellations? _____

2. Orion is visible at what time of the year? _____

3. Why is the moon in a different place each night? _____

_____

Metaphor

Metaphors are comparisons similar to similes. The difference is that a metaphor does not use any clue words (whereas the simile uses "like" or "as").

Explain what is being compared in each sentence.

1. His grandfather is a pack rat. _____

_____

2. That man is a volcano ready to explode. _____

_____

3. Her eyes were fireworks. _____

_____

4. Joseph is a worm for how he treated his mother. _____

_____

5. Schools plant the seeds of wisdom. _____

_____

6. The test was a piece of cake. _____

_____

7. He showered her with gifts. _____

_____

Find the word in the group which is not spelled correctly.

1. maintain	bachelor	canceled	comitted
2. safetey	relevant	restrain	department
3. vacation	beautiful	reletive	repair
4. objection	cabbage	wheather	aboard
5. personel	support	company	command
6. Tuesday	Wendsday	Thursday	Saturday
7. through	thought	throne	throughn
8. teacher	agread	thread	cheap
9. yesterday	village	question	arithmatic
10. breakfest	baking	surface	regular
11. December	November	Feburary	January
12. kitchen	remember	perfect	animel
13. address	weather	cieties	whether
14. uncle	guilty	grieff	judge
15. select	repair	trouble	caried

For some operations with fractions it helps to rewrite the fractions as mixed numbers or rewrite mixed numbers as fractions. To rewrite a mixed number, first multiply the denominator by the whole number. Next add the numerator to the product. Finally, write that sum above the denominator.

Example: $4 \dfrac{3}{8}$	Step 1. 4 x 8 = 32	Step 2. 32 + 3 = 35	Step 3. $\dfrac{35}{8}$

1. $3 \dfrac{2}{3}$ 2. $4 \dfrac{3}{5}$ 3. $1 \dfrac{5}{7}$ 4. $3 \dfrac{5}{6}$ 5. $7 \dfrac{3}{4}$

To change an improper fraction to a mixed number, reverse the steps.

Example: $\dfrac{35}{8}$	35 ÷ 8 = 4 r 3	The quotient becomes the whole number and the remainder becomes the numerator.	$\dfrac{43}{8}$

6. $\dfrac{5}{2}$ 7. $\dfrac{41}{7}$ 8. $\dfrac{32}{7}$ 9. $\dfrac{13}{9}$ 10. $\dfrac{25}{8}$

Choose your STRENGTH exercise!

Exercise for today:

_____

Check & Record in Fitness Log.

Day 9

SELF-DISCIPLINE

SELF DISCIPLINE - Jackie Robinson

Value

If someone calls us a name, we feel justified in reacting. We often call the other person a name, or talk about them to our friends. It's very difficult to practice self-discipline – to keep ourselves in control.

Jackie Robinson was a baseball player. He was the first African American to play major league baseball. He had been playing in the Negro league, because in 1944, the baseball leagues were segregated. Branch Rickey, vice president of the Brooklyn Dodgers, wanted to change that and enlisted Robinson for that purpose. He made Robinson promise that he would not fight back when confronted with racism.

Players from other teams objected to playing against Robinson. Many fans jeered him. He and his family received threats. Some of his teammates threatened to sit out, but Manager Leo Durocher said he would trade them before he would trade Robinson. His faith in Robinson, coupled with Robinson's great athletic talent, and the self-discipline he employed to rise above the persecution, finally persuaded people to look beyond his color. He is considered by many to be one of baseball's greatest players.

1. What does it mean to say "the baseball leagues were segregated?" _____

_____

2. What was the position of Branch Rickey with the Dodgers baseball team? _____

_____

3. What promise did Rickey insist Robinson make? _____

_____

4. In addition to self-discipline, what qualities did Robinson employ to deal positively with the racism that he encountered? _____

_____

_____

Value: SELF-DISCIPLINE

FAMILY ACTIVITIES

Choose one or more activities to do with your family or friends.

Let's talk about it...

Encourage your child to be determined and focused when completing a task or project. Identify a project or sport that your child has not done such as swimming, playing basketball, or tennis. Introduce him/her to it and encourage them to stay involved for a certain amount of time.

 Plan to exercise together as a family this week. Have a family walk after dinner. Choose an activity to do together. Hike, bike, swim, dance and play together. At night, play a game of "flashlight tag." Whoever gets "tagged" by the light is "it."

 Give up TV for a day, a week, or longer. Instead, spend time outside, reading, or with family and friends.

 Plan a sequence of events or activities to do in one day. Before you move on to the next one you must finish the one before it.

VALUES ARE A FAMILY AFFAIR

 Read more about
SELF-DISCIPLINE

Hatchet
By Gary Paulsen

Beyond the Divide
By Kathryn Lasky

Runaway
By Wendelin Van Draanen

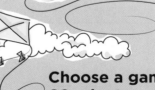

Choose a game or activity to play for 60 minutes as a family or with friends today!

 Day 10

Choose a **Play** or **Exercise** Activity!

INCENTIVE CONTRACT CALENDAR

My parents and I agree that if I complete this section of

Summer Fit Activities™

and read _____ minutes a day, my reward will be _____

Child Signature: _____   Parent Signature: _____

Day 1			Day 6		
Day 2			Day 7		
Day 3			Day 8		
Day 4			Day 9		
Day 5			Day 10		

Color the for each day of activities completed.

Color the for each day of reading completed.

Summer Fitness Log

Choose your exercise activity each day from the Aerobic and Strength Activities in the back of the book. Record the date, stretch, activity and how long you performed your exercise activity below. Fill in how many days you complete your fitness activity on your Incentive Contract Calendars.

	Date	Stretch	Activity	Time
examples:	June 4	Run in place	Sky Reach	7 min
	June 5	Toe Touches	Bottle Curls	15 min
1.				
2.				
3.				
4.				
5.				
6.				
7.				
8.				
9.				
10.				

I promise to do my best for me. I exercise to be healthy and active. I am awesome because I am me.

Child Signature: _____

1. $\dfrac{1}{3} + \dfrac{1}{3} = \dfrac{2}{3}$

2. $\dfrac{3}{8} + \dfrac{2}{8} = \dfrac{5}{8}$

3. $\dfrac{8}{9} + \dfrac{2}{9} = \dfrac{10}{9}$

4. $\dfrac{4}{7} + \dfrac{5}{7} = \dfrac{9}{7}$

5. $\dfrac{10}{27} - \dfrac{4}{27} = \dfrac{6}{27}$

6. $\dfrac{9}{20} - \dfrac{3}{20} = \dfrac{6}{20}$

7. $\dfrac{4}{5} - \dfrac{2}{5} =$

8. $\dfrac{9}{15} - \dfrac{4}{15} =$

9. $\dfrac{7}{19} + \dfrac{1}{19} + \dfrac{7}{19} =$

10. $\dfrac{11}{15} + \dfrac{2}{15} + \dfrac{8}{15} =$

Comprehension

The boys had been working all day. They were sweaty and dirty. Their hands had blisters from swinging the small ax and using the hammers, but they felt a great sense of accomplishment.

They were now the proud owners of a tree fort. They had spent days discussing the elements they wanted to include – two levels, a moat on one side of the tree, a tunnel leading from the base of the tree to a spot about 50 feet out. They had compromised a bit on the tunnel – it wasn't actually dug out of the ground. Instead, they had cleared the ground for the distance needed, then arranged branches to form the roof of the tunnel. They had to look quite a while to find enough curved branches to achieve this, but they did it.

The ladder was "borrowed" from Owen's garage. Tyler had supplied the planks for the floor by tearing apart an old, decrepit shed behind his home. Ahmed had requested the necessary nails from his dad, who had been reading the paper and only half heard what was said to him.

They had brought sandwiches for lunch, but now they were really hungry. It was getting dark and they knew they needed to go home, get dinner, and sleep, but they were reluctant to leave. So for a while, they just sat in the fort, listening to the noises of evening coming on, and enjoying their achievement.

1. What were the extra elements of the fort? _____

_____

2. Why were the boys reluctant to go home? _____

_____

3. Define the word decrepit_____

_____

4. What supplies did the boys need for their construction? _____

_____

5. Why would a group of kids want a tree fort?_____

_____

Intensive pronouns

Intensive pronouns are the words *myself, yourself, himself, herself, itself, ourselves, yourselves, themselves*. When they are used to emphasize the subject of the sentence, usually appearing right next to the subject, they are called intensive. (These same words are reflexive pronouns when they refer to the subject, but not emphasize it, as in *I gave myself a present*.)

Circle the intensive pronoun in each sentence.

1. The teacher told the student, "You yourself need to do all the work on this project."
2. I myself am tired of standing in line.
3. The hawk itself caught a rabbit.
4. The soldiers themselves marched in the parade.
5. The artist herself signed the painting.
6. We ourselves decided to put on a show.
7. My grandfather himself met John F. Kennedy.
8. We ourselves had nothing to do with the mess in the kitchen.
9. Mom told us, "You yourselves need to get your laundry put away."
10. We ourselves made all the food for the party.

The Reason for Seasons

We live in the Northern Hemisphere. It is summer when the North Pole is tilted toward the sun. At this time, the sun is high overhead and we receive strong sun rays. The sun shines for many hours each day. Its strong rays have a lot of time to heat Earth. In the far North, the sun shines for 24 hours a day. This gradually changes. Days get shorter and cooler, and the sun appears low in the sky at noon as the North Pole moves slowly away from the sun. Summer turns to fall, and then to winter. In winter, the North Pole is tilted away from the sun. We do not receive the strong rays and the sun is low in the sky. The sun shines for fewer hours each day. These weak rays do not have time to heat Earth. This explains the colder winters even though the sun is shining. Winter turns to spring and then back to summer as Earth completes one journey around the sun.

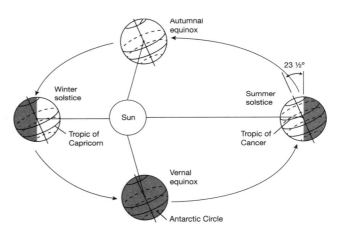

Choose your **STRENGTH** exercise!

Exercise for today:

Check & Record in Fitness Log.

Day 1

Add/Subtract fractions with unlike denominators

First remember to find the LCD and make equivalent fractions before adding or subtracting.

Example $\dfrac{1}{2} + \dfrac{1}{3} + \dfrac{1}{4} = \dfrac{6}{12} + \dfrac{4}{12} + \dfrac{3}{12} = \dfrac{13}{12} = 1\dfrac{1}{12}$

1. $\dfrac{8}{9} - \dfrac{5}{6} =$

2. $\dfrac{7}{8} + \dfrac{3}{5} =$

3. $\dfrac{7}{8} - \dfrac{2}{3} =$

4. $\dfrac{5}{9} + \dfrac{4}{27} =$

5. $\dfrac{9}{10} - \dfrac{2}{3} =$

6. $\dfrac{1}{9} + \dfrac{5}{6} =$

Feudalism

In Europe, you will find many rivers. During the middle ages, these rivers helped warring people enter European countries and try to conquer them. People began to group together, supporting one another, to repel the invaders. A system developed which was an agreement among the kings, lords, and knights. We call it the feudal system.

In the feudal system, the knights were vassals. A vassal is a person who serves someone else (in fact, the word vassal means servant). The knights would serve a noble or lord. They would be available when needed to protect the lord or his lands. In return, the knights would receive land of their own. A knight could be a vassal for more than one lord. This only worked as long as the lords he worked for didn't fight with each other!

The lords were vassals, too – they were vassals of the king. They had to support and protect the king.

There was another group of people at that time, but they were not really part of the feudal system, these were the peasants. They worked the land for the lords or the knights. There was the understanding that the lord or knight would protect them in case of attack. The peasants would grow the crops and tend the animals. They sometimes had a small plot of land for themselves.

1. Which group of people were not technically part of the feudal system?_____

_____

2. What was the agreement between the lords and the knights (what did each one get out of the system?) _____

_____

_____

_____

3. What does the word vassal mean? _____

_____

_____

There are words that sound the same but have different spellings. The correct spelling is important to the reader, because the spelling denotes the correct meaning. In the following sentences, circle the correct word to fit in sentence.

1. I could not see (threw , through) the curtain, so I missed the sunrise.

2. Javier did not want to (waste, waist) the delicious dinner, so he got a to-go box.

3. Many people are worried that global warming will cause (holes , wholes) in the ozone layer.

4. It was to (their , they're , there) advantage to get to the movie early.

5. Did you have to (weight , wait) long to buy your tickets?

6. There was a great (sail , sale) at the game store.

7. Did you decide (witch , which) costume you want to use for Halloween?

8. He looked outside to get an idea of what the (weather , whether) would be for the day.

9. Stefan was unhappy that he placed (forth , fourth) in the race.

10. Bonita and Allen said (their , they're, there) going to meet us at the mall.

11. Karl was so hungry that he ate the (hole , whole) pizza himself.

12. Please put the flower vase over (their , they're , there) on the coffee table.

13. Football players sometimes like to put on more (wait , weight) so they have more power.

14. Selena could not decide (weather , whether) or not to take French.

15. Hiekoti (threw , through) the football as hard as he could.

Water Cycle

The earth has a limited amount of water. So the water keeps recycling. We begin with the water in rivers, lakes, and oceans. The sun heats the water, turning it into vapor or steam. This goes into the air (a process called evaporation). When the water vapor in the air gets cold, condensation occurs, causing the vapor to form clouds. When the clouds have so much condensed water that they can't hold any more, we get precipitation (rain or snow). This falls to the earth and is collected back into the oceans, lakes and rivers. Where it falls to the ground, it will soak into the earth and become ground water. This is called the water cycle because it just keeps repeating.

Draw a diagram of the water cycle on a separate piece of paper. Be sure to include and correctly label evaporation, condensation, precipitation, and collection.

Choose your **AEROBIC** exercise!

Exercise for today:

Check & Record in Fitness Log.

Day 2

Historical Fiction

Historical fiction is a genre of literature which places a fictional story in a real time period of history in a realistic manner. Often this type of story helps the reader to understand the real historical events because they can identify with the characters in the story. You may have read Number the Stars, The Shakespeare Stealer, or Al Capone Does My Shirts. (If not, you may want to – they're very good books.)

Read the situations below. Decide if each one would be an example of historical fiction or not. If you think it is, mark it with a **Y**; if not, mark it with an **N**.

1. _____ Billy and his sister Veronica were headed into the mountains to look for berries. Berries were a nice, sweet treat after dinner, and when they were in season, the two brought home as many as they could. They had to be careful, however. When climbing around in the mountains, they might disturb some of the animals that made the mountains their home. That wasn't a problem if it was just some bluebirds, or small rodents. But if it were a mountain lion or a dinosaur, even a baby one, that could be very dangerous. They were glad they had found the dinosaurs stun guns in the market the last time they had flown to town, but weren't sure they really wanted to try them out.

2. _____ Francine and Amanda skipped along the dirt road, holding the large basket between them. They really enjoyed going to the market for their mother. They got to see all the new things that the merchants had gotten in on the latest ships. They sometimes got to visit with their friends. They were able to listen to the grown-ups gossip and talk politics (if they stayed quiet enough to not be noticed.) That was how they had heard about the Battle of Bunker Hill. They had listened to the grown-ups tell the stories, then rushed home to tell their parents.

3. _____ Kano loved his home along the Nile. It was such a big, beautiful river. He loved to watch the boats passing by, especially the Pharaoh's boats. They were so large and colorful. Once he even thought he saw the Pharaoh and the young prince.

4. _____ Nancy was very quiet leaving the house. If Mother heard her, she wouldn't be allowed to go. But it was all she had thought about for weeks. All the colorful banners, the interesting people, and all the unique animals! But most of all, she wanted to listen to the elucidators – the people who had come to share their knowledge of magic. She wanted to learn the spells to help her family's cow produce more milk, and make their garden grow more prolifically, and most of all, the spell to make her sister learn how to behave.

5. _____ Two nights to go. Two more nights and Paul's brother should be home. Paul wasn't sure why his brother had thought it so important to go to war. Paul didn't think it should be their fight. Yes, they lived in the South, and people said slavery was important to the economy. But Paul's family had never had slaves. They didn't believe in holding another human being in bondage. So Paul couldn't understand why Christopher had left to fight for the Confederate Army. But he didn't care anymore. Christopher would be home tomorrow and everything would be like it was before the war.

Connecting words, also called transition words, are very important to the skill of writing. They serve a variety of purposes. They connect ideas, and also stress differences. They can indicate agreement, disagreement, results, and conclusions. They can also help keep the sequence of events clear. Circle the transition words in these sentences. Remember sometimes it is a phrase rather than just one word.

1. She wanted the shoes as well as the purse.
2. They wanted to sleep late on Saturday, however, the ball game was at 8:00.
3. Francois first went to the doctor; then he went to the pharmacist.
4. They were gone a long time, but when they returned, they were very happy.
5. Alice wanted a popsicle instead of an ice cream bar.
6. Anthony found the clue first, then he was able to find the hidden treasure.
7. They had to come home early because of the rain.
8. To summarize, there were eight members of the group present.
9. Caroline washed the dishes in addition to sweeping the floor.
10. Jim, together with Jennifer, decided to apply for positions as camp counselors.
11. They went to sleep right away, although none of the children thought they were tired.
12. Despite the storm warnings that had been broadcast, many were caught in the bad weather.
13. Tony learned to always have his phone with him, in case of emergency.
14. The family decided that, all things considered, it had been a good vacation.

Add/Subtract mixed numbers

Adding or subtracting the whole numbers is done like you normally do. Remember that to add or subtract the fraction part, the fractions need a common denominator.

Example
$$6 \frac{1}{3} = 6 \frac{5}{15}$$
$$+ 5 \frac{2}{5} = 5 \frac{6}{15}$$
$$\overline{11 \frac{11}{15}}$$

1.
$$11 \frac{2}{3}$$
$$- 7 \frac{3}{5}$$

2.
$$3 \frac{1}{10}$$
$$+ 5 \frac{3}{4}$$

Choose your STRENGTH exercise!

Exercise for today:

Day 3

Check & Record in Fitness Log.

Metaphor is a very effective tool in poetry. The device allows the poet to create an image through the metaphor that looks at something in a very unique way. Consider the poem Fog by Carl Sandburg.

> **FOG**
>
> The fog comes
> on little cat feet.
>
> It sits looking
> over harbor and city
>
> on silent haunches
> and then moves on.

You can imagine fog moving in the way a cat does. It is silent, as a cat often is. It creeps in and then moves on when it is ready.

Try to think of a metaphor for some ordinary things. In each case, explain how the original item and the metaphor are the same.

1. Paper _____

_____

2. Night _____

_____

3. Time _____

_____

4. A shadow _____

_____

5. A playground _____

_____

6. Your best friend _____

_____

7. Your room _____

_____

Pronouns in verb agreement

In a sentence, your subject and verb need to agree – a singular subject needs a singular verb. You would not say "They is happy," you would say "They are happy." You are probably familiar enough with most pronouns to be accurate, but indefinite pronouns cause a little confusion. These pronouns are singular: each, either, neither, one, anyone, everyone, someone, anybody, everybody, and somebody. These are plural: both, few, many, several. These can be singular or plural, depending on the noun to which they refer: all, any, most, none, some.

Circle the correct form of the verb for use in each of these sentences.

1. One of the children (is , are) sure that the books were turned in.
2. Many of them (is , are) worried about having too much homework over the weekend.
3. Somebody (has , have) left their locker open.
4. All of the musicians (says , say) that they are ready for the concert.
5. (Is , Are) there anyone ready to present their paper?
6. Anybody (is , are) welcome to participate in the history fair.
7. Each of the onlookers (remember , remembers) the situation differently.
8. Every one of Mary's friends (want , wants) her party to be a success.
9. Several of the animals (was , were) out of their cages.
10. Carol says they (play , plays) that song on the radio every day.
11. Some of the book (has , have) been read aloud to the children.
12. Some of the stories (has , have) been altered.
13. Neither person (is , was) willing to accept responsibility.
14. Both Marcella and Henry (believes , believe) Angela's story.

Multiply simple fractions **Multiply the numerators; multiply the denominators; simplify.**

Example $\dfrac{5}{6} \times \dfrac{2}{3} = \dfrac{10}{18} = \dfrac{5}{9}$

1. $\dfrac{5}{6} \times \dfrac{1}{5} = \dfrac{5}{30} = \dfrac{1}{6}$

2. $\dfrac{2}{5} \times \dfrac{3}{4} = \dfrac{6}{20} = \dfrac{3}{10}$

3. $\dfrac{5}{7} \times \dfrac{7}{9} = \dfrac{35}{63} = \dfrac{5}{9}$

4. $\dfrac{1}{5} \times \dfrac{1}{3} = \dfrac{1}{15} = \dfrac{1}{15}$

Choose your AEROBIC exercise!

Exercise for today:

Check & Record in Fitness Log.

Day 4

KINDNESS

KINDNESS - Oral Lee Brown

Value

Oral Lee Brown grew up in poverty. She struggled as a mother of three to make ends meet. She rose above her circumstances, owning a real estate office and a restaurant. She even created a popular peach cobbler dessert, which she marketed, but she believed in giving something back.

Through a chance encounter with a little girl in a grocery store in 1987, she became acquainted with Brookfield Elementary School in East Oakland California. She decided to "adopt" the class of 23 first graders. She told the children that if they stayed in school, she would pay for their college – and she began to put about ¼ of her salary into a savings account right then. She made regular visits to the school, helped tutor, met with parents, bought supplies, and tracked the children's progress.

19 of those children graduated college in 2003 and 2004. Three others went into trade schools. But Mrs. Brown's kindness did not end with those children. She has gone on to sponsor 5 more classes and more than 125 children. Helping others is the legacy of kindness given by Oral Lee Brown.

1. What is a synonym for poverty? _____

_____

2. What are three things that Oral Lee did that showed success:_____

_____

_____

_____

3. How much of her salary did Oral Lee set aside to help the children of Brookfield

Elementary School? _____

_____

4. How did the children demonstrate that they appreciated Oral Lee's sacrifice for them?

_____

_____

Value: KINDNESS

FAMILY ACTIVITIES

Choose one or more activities to do with your family or friends.

 Play "10 good things" with your friends or family. Pick a person and tell 10 nice things about them.

 Write notes to your neighbors thanking them for being good neighbors.

 Have a lemonade stand and donate the money you earn to a food bank or homeless shelter.

 Collect toys, books, and games you no longer play with and donate them.

Let's talk about it...

Children learn what they live, if they see you practicing random acts of kindness, they will want to do them too. Discuss things your family can do together to help others. Set aside some time to volunteer at a soup kitchen or homeless shelter. Remind your child that kindness begins with a smile and should be practiced at home too!

VALUES ARE A FAMILY AFFAIR

 Read more about **KINDNESS**

Ruined
By Paula Morris

The Terrible Wave
By Marden Dahlstedt

Jane Addams
By Mary Kittredge

Choose a game or activity to play for 60 minutes as a family or with friends today!

Day 5

Choose a Play or Exercise Activity!

6-7 • © Summer Fit Activities™

Summer Explorer

Healthy Planet Activities and Fun Things to Do!

- Create a summer "Bucket List".

- Make a friendship bracelet for the planet.

- Go to a summer blockbuster movie.

- Make ice cream sandwiches.

- Instead of asking for a ride, walk or ride your bike.

- Learn how to cook something new and cook dinner for your family.

- Write a play.

- Go to a farmer's market and learn about something that is grown or made in your area.

- Have a food drive for a local food bank.

- Paint a self-portrait.

- Think of something you do well, now teach your skill to someone.

- Organize a neighborhood garbage walk to pick up trash and clean up your neighborhood.

- Visit a local nature preserve.

- Choose an animal to study. Create a presentation and take it to your local zoo to display.

- Host a board game night.

- Make a robot or other creation out of items from your recycle bin.

- Visit a bank in your neighborhood, learn about the services they offer. Think about opening a savings account.

Recyclable Creations "Junk Monsters"

 Gather clean cans, bottles, and boxes from recycling bin.

 Use plastic lids, newspaper strips, nuts, screws, buttons, pipe cleaners, rubber bands to make faces, and arms and legs. Your parents will need to help you glue with a hot glue gun.

 Create monsters, robots, or your family members!

Summer Journal III

Write about your best friend, brother or sister.

The Renaissance began partly as a result of the trade between the Far East and Mediterranean cities. The traders brought spices and gold from the East, but they also brought information about different cultures. Marco Polo, an Italian merchant, lived in the Orient for many years and wrote about his experiences. When he returned, he not only brought goods to trade, but ideas to share. This exchange of ideas and goods is part of the geographic theme of movement.

During the Renaissance, new ideas in many fields of thought abounded. Artists began to try new media, and new techniques. Philosophers looked at ancient history and philosophy, then took those ideas and infused them with renewed interest and new insights. Advances were made in medicine and science. New instruments, techniques, and theories led to growth in the area of exploration.

The Medici family was wealthy and powerful. They became patrons of the arts in Florence, Italy. A patron would basically hire an artist to work for only him. The artist would design and paint chapels and rooms, carve statues for decoration, and paint beautiful pictures for the patron.

One well-known scientist of the time was Galileo Galilei. He invented telescopes, a compass, and a thermometer. With the use of the telescopes, he was a ground breaking astronomer. He observed and noted four of Jupiter's moons.

Prince Henry of Portugal is also referred to as Prince Henry the Navigator. His contributions to the Renaissance included starting a school for oceanic navigation. He supported many explorers as they tried to find an ocean path around Africa.

What three things are mentioned as being brought back from the Far East by the traders?

1. _____

2. _____

3. _____

Divide fractions To divide by a fraction, multiply by the reciprocal of the divisor. Remember that the reciprocal is the fraction turned upside down. To divide a fraction by a whole number, change the whole number to an improper fraction. **Use a separate piece of paper to work the problems below.**

Ex: $\dfrac{5}{8} \div \dfrac{3}{8} = \dfrac{5}{8} \times \dfrac{8}{3} = \dfrac{40}{24} = \dfrac{5}{3} = 1\dfrac{2}{3}$

$\dfrac{2}{3} \div 4 = \dfrac{2}{3} \div \dfrac{4}{1} = \dfrac{2}{3} \times \dfrac{1}{4} = \dfrac{2}{12} = \dfrac{1}{6}$

1. $\dfrac{3}{4} \div \dfrac{1}{2} =$

2. $\dfrac{2}{3} \div \dfrac{3}{4} =$

3. $5 \div \dfrac{5}{8} =$

Prepositions are words that show a relationship between other words. One way to look at it is the relationship between a fox and a log. The fox can go through the log, over it, around it, under it, near it, or in it, to list a few. There are some prepositions that don't work with the fox, such as during, after, except, about, and among. There are also some prepositions made up of more than one word, such as according to, in addition to, on account of and in spite of.

In the following sentences, circle the prepositional phrases.

1. The rabbit ran into the huge garden.

2. The little girl stood on the chair so she could see.

3. The book is always better than the movie according to some people.

4. The boys picked up trash in addition to raking the yard.

5. The dog lay between the flower garden and the little pond.

Rewrite these sentences, adding a prepositional phrase to each.

6. The cat ate her dinner. _____

_____

_____

7. Gabrielle is practicing her guitar. _____

_____

_____

8. Abram did his work. _____

_____

_____

9. Bill read the newspaper. _____

_____

_____

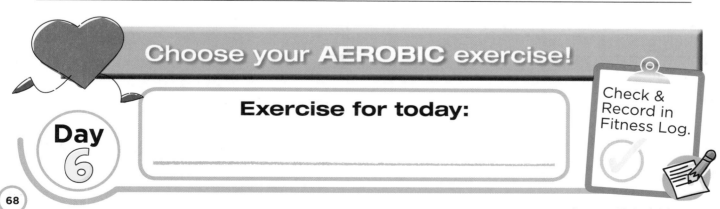

Choose your **AEROBIC** exercise!

Exercise for today:

Check & Record in Fitness Log.

Day 6

Division of Mixed Numbers

Divide mixed numbers To divide with a mixed number, change the mixed number to an improper fraction.

1. $\dfrac{3}{4} \div 6\dfrac{1}{2} =$

2. $9\dfrac{1}{2} \div \dfrac{6}{8} =$

3. $5\dfrac{1}{4} \div 2\dfrac{5}{8} =$

4. $5\dfrac{1}{4} \div 3\dfrac{3}{8} =$

5. $3\dfrac{1}{2} \div 2\dfrac{3}{5} =$

6. $7\dfrac{1}{2} \div 3\dfrac{3}{4} =$

Gravity

Gravity attracts all objects towards each other. Gravity has been around since the very beginning of the universe, and it works the same way everywhere in the universe, on all kinds of different objects, of all different sizes. The bigger an object is, and the closer you are to it, the stronger its gravitational pull is.

In the very beginning of the universe, gravity pulled atoms together to make stars and planets. Once the stars and planets had formed, gravity kept the planets in orbit around the stars, and moons orbiting around the planets. On each planet that is large enough, gravity keeps an atmosphere around the planet.

On Earth, gravity keeps the air around us (and everything else) from drifting off into space. Gravity also causes things to fall to the ground, causes the ocean's tides, and causes hot air to rise while colder air falls (which in turn causes wind). Gravity is everywhere!

1. _____ attracts all objects towards each other.

2. Gravity works everywhere in the _____.

3. In the beginning, gravity pulled atoms together to make the _____ and the planets.

4. Gravity keeps the planets in _____ around the stars, and _____ in orbit around the planets.

5. Gravity keeps an _____ around planets that are large enough.

6. On _____, gravity keeps us from drifting off into space.

A compound sentence is one that has two or more simple sentences, usually joined by a connecting word. Sometimes an author uses sentences or varying lengths to make the writing interesting. The words used as connectors, or conjunctions, for compound sentences are: for, and, nor, but, or, yet, so. Except for very short sentences, a comma comes before the conjunction. **Use conjunctions to make each pair of short sentences one compound sentence.**

1. I do not like snakes. My friend, Alejandro, is very interested in them. _____

_____

_____

2. Carlos helped the younger children at recess. Carrie helped them after school. _____

_____

_____

3. My friend and I built a doghouse. The dog would not stay in it. _____

_____

_____

4. I tried to speak French. My friend tried to speak Chinese. _____

_____

_____

5. Kathleen forgot her lunch. She called her mother. _____

_____

_____

6. Robert threw his football across the room. Andrew caught it. _____

_____

_____

Choose your STRENGTH exercise!

Exercise for today:

Check & Record in Fitness Log.

Day 7

6-7 • © Summer Fit Activities™

Ratio

A **ratio** is a comparison of two quantities. It can be written more than one way, but they are read the same way. If a ratio is written 2 : 3, you would read it, "Two to three". Another way to write a ratio is as a fraction, which may or may not be reduced to lowest terms.

Mrs. B's class	Boys	Girls	Total
7th Grade	18	15	33
8th Grade	16	19	35
In Band	7	8	15
In Basketball	21	20	41
In Volleyball	15	17	32

If there are 18 boys in a class, and 19 girls, the ratio of boys to girls is 18 : 19.

Use the chart to write some ratios.

1) The ratio of boys to girls in band class is _____

2) The ratio of 7th graders to 8th graders is _____

3) The ratio of girls to boys in 8th grade is _____

4) The ratio of 8th graders to 7th graders is _____

5) The ratio of boys to girls in volleyball is _____

Challenge: What ratio could you simplify to have a final answer of 6 : 5? _____

Industrial Revolution

As people began to move from the country to the cities and towns, many people worked in their own homes, this was called Cottage Industry. Many women were part of the textile industry – spinning cotton into thread. A man named James Hargreaves invented a hand-powered spinning machine, that was a great improvement over the traditional spinning wheel. This allowed weavers to work faster, therefore increasing production. Factories were built beginning around the 1750s in England.

Factories were able to produce goods faster than the skilled craftsmen, and they could produce them for less money. People began to leave the cottage industries and work in the factories. Some of the advantages were that they didn't have to have their own equipment, they could leave their work at the end of the day, their pay was more secure (they didn't have to wait until a product was finished and hope the person who ordered it still wanted it).

There were disadvantages as well. The people in the factories worked long hours, in difficult conditions, and for little pay. Children often worked as long as adults in order to help their families have enough money to live.

An interesting note is that the early factories needed running water to power the machinery. So the manufacturers followed the example of the early civilizations, and settled near rivers.

1. Where did the early manufacturers have to build their factories? _____

_____

2. What were three disadvantages of working in the factories? _____

_____

Idioms in Literature

Authors often include idioms in their work in order to make it more interesting. An idiom is a word or phrase that cannot be taken literally. Sometimes using an idiom explains a situation more clearly and easily than writing out an explanation.

Match the following idioms to their meanings.

1. _____ His bark is worse than his bite.   A. Trick someone

2. _____ Pull the wool over his eyes.   B. Mischief

3. _____ Every dog has his day.   C. Everyone will have an opportunity.

4. _____ Monkey business   D. He sounds meaner than he is.

5. _____ In a pickle   E. Get it exactly right.

6. _____ When pigs fly   F. In a difficult situation

7. _____ Hit the nail on the head   G. Seem funny to someone

8. _____ The buck stops here.   H. Will never happen

9. _____ A flash in the pan   I. I take responsibility for this.

10. _____ Strike someone funny   J. Something that looks great, but doesn't work out

Write an explanation for each of the following idioms.

11. The nick of time _____

12. Bite off more than you can chew _____

13. Hit the bull's eye _____

14. Fill someone's shoes _____

15. Curiosity killed the cat _____

16. Blow off steam _____

17. Clear as a bell _____

18. Eyes are bigger than your stomach _____

Choose your AEROBIC exercise!

Exercise for today:

_____

Check & Record in Fitness Log.

Day 8

SummerFitActivities.com

Day 9

Proportion

An equation which states that two ratios are equal is called a proportion. There are two ways to write a proportion. This proportion is read, "40 is to 5 as 48 is to 6."

$$40 : 5 = 48 : 6 \qquad\qquad \frac{40}{5} = \frac{48}{6}$$

Write these situations as ratios. If they are equal, circle the ratio. They are equal if they form an equivalent fraction.

1. 75 correct out of 100
    150 correct out of 200

2. 15 out of 30 students
    25 out of 45 students

To solve a proportion, complete two equal ratios.

| Example | $\frac{30}{45}$ | = | $\frac{6}{n}$ | $\frac{30 \div 5}{45 \div 5}$ | = | $\frac{6}{9}$ | or 30 ÷ 6 = 5, so you must divide 45 by 5 to find n. |

3. $\dfrac{3}{6} = \dfrac{n}{36}$

4. $\dfrac{56}{64} = \dfrac{7}{n}$

5. $\dfrac{8}{5} = \dfrac{24}{n}$

6. $\dfrac{27}{33} = \dfrac{n}{11}$

Observatories

An observatory is a place where very large and powerful telescopes are used to see into and study outer space. See if you can find the following words in the word search:

```
m  r  m  s  s  p  a  c  e  s
s  n  e  n  r  o  m  p  p  u
a  s  t  r  o  n  o  m  y  n
t  r  e  s  m  c  s  y  e  a
u  a  o  a  s  p  t  r  o  r
r  t  r  e  t  i  p  u  j  u
n  s  l  r  u  l  s  c  r  e
n  e  p  t  u  n  e  r  e  y
t  e  v  t  s  u  n  e  v  v
n  o  o  m  u  t  u  m  c  r
```

Astronomy	Moon	Space
Jupiter	Neptune	Stars
Mars	Pluto	Uranus
Mercury	Telescope	Venus
Meteor	Saturn	

Common Spelling Mistakes

- Lose means to misplace something – Loose is the opposite of tight (Loose has room for 2 O's)
- Your means something belongs to you - You're, the apostrophe means a letter is missing (you are)
- Accept means to receive willingly – Except means to leave out
- It's, again the apostrophe shows something missing (It is) – Its means belonging to it
- Affect is a verb, meaning to act upon – Effect is a noun, the result of something
- Then means in the past- Than is a comparison (he is taller than she is)
- Weird breaks the rule of i before e – because it's weird
- A lot is NOT one word – it is two words
- Passed means to go by something or someone – Past means it has already happened.

Choose the correct words in the following paragraph.

Georgia was ready to (accept , except) her award. She was proud of the (affect , effect) her composition had on her classmates. She hoped (alot , a lot) of them would come to the presentation. It might be a little (wierd , weird) to be on stage in front of everyone, but she'd deal with it. It would be easier (than , then) doing a song and dance, for sure. She (passed , past) Abby on the way to the auditorium. She said hello and thought it would be really awkward to (loose , lose) her speech at this time. Then, she stepped on the stage to have her moment in the sun.

Adjectives

Adjectives are words that describe nouns or pronouns. They are often descriptive words, but can also be words that tell how many. Adjectives can also compare one noun or pronoun to another. These adjectives are positive (describing one thing), comparative (comparing two) or superlative (comparing three or more). Circle the adjective in each sentence.

1. My cute kitty is washing her face.
2. Max cooked a peppery sauce.
3. The windmill made a screechy sound.
4. Edna has the best race time of anyone.
5. I will be more careful than Marta.
6. Of the two of you, I hope the better person wins.
7. My cold is worse than Jerry's.
8. Black soot covered the chimney.
9. The cows went into the empty barn.
10. She danced in a shimmery dress.
11. There were nine boys in the class.
12. The guitar had a beautiful design.
13. The huge box waited to be opened.
14. Hank's chair was the most comfortable one in the house.
15. The blinding light gave him a headache.

Choose your **STRENGTH** exercise!

Exercise for today:

Check & Record in Fitness Log.

Day 9

COURAGE

COURAGE - Christa McAuliffe

Value

Courage can be defined as the ability to confront fear, pain, danger or uncertainty.

Christa McAuliffe was a teacher. Teaching is not a profession normally associated with courage. McAuliffe, however, was posthumously awarded the Congressional Space Medal of Honor. Pretty impressive for a teacher!

McAuliffe taught history, social studies, and civics in a junior high school. She developed and taught a course on "The American Woman." She also volunteered in her church, was a girl scout leader and raised funds for hospitals and the YMCA.

In 1984, along with 11,000 others, McAuliffe applied to NASA to be a "Teacher in Space." NASA's plan was to find a gifted teacher who could communicate to children from space. Although the space program had been in place since the 1960s, there were still dangers associated with space travel. McAuliffe knew this, but volunteered anyway. She faced the dangers and the uncertainties with a positive attitude, certain that she would be helping students. The space shuttle Challenger was launched on January 28, 1986, but exploded after the launch, killing all those aboard.

McAuliffe's example has led others to continue her quest. In 2004, Teachers in Space, a non-profit project sponsored by the Space Frontier Foundation began a project to again try to send teachers into space, to inspire and encourage young people's interest in space exploration.

1. Define posthumously: _____

2. Why is the Space Frontier Foundation trying to send teachers into space? _____

_____

_____

3. Find a word in the story that is a synonym for perspective. _____

4. Find a word in the story that is an antonym for safety. _____

5. What were some of the ordinary, non-courageous, things that McAuliffe did with her life?

_____

_____

_____

Value: COURAGE

FAMILY ACTIVITIES

Choose one or more activities to do with your family or friends.

 As a family, watch a movie that demonstrates courage such as *Charlotte's Web*, *The Sound of Music*, *The Wizard of Oz*, *The Lion King*, *ET*, or *Finding Nemo*. Discuss how the characters in the movie display courage. What might have happened if they hadn't been courageous?

 Make and decorate a pennant for your room that says "I believe in myself." Discuss with your parents how being the best you can be is an act of courage.

 Talk about the courage it takes for a blind person to get through the day. Take turns blindfolding each other and try to do your everyday things. Ask your parents to help you look up the story of Ben Underwood, a blind teen who rides a skateboard and plays video games.

 Think about the most courageous person you know. Write about how they demonstrate courage.

Let's talk about it...

Courage is something built over time. Discuss everyday situations with your child and the opportunities they have to be brave. Read books about people who display courage. Encourage them to share their fears and brainstorm together ways to face and overcome those fears. Talk with them about a time you were afraid but found the courage to get through.

VALUES ARE A FAMILY AFFAIR

Read more about COURAGE

Alice the Brave
By Phyllis Reynolds Naylor

Red Cap
By G. Clifton Wisler

Steal Away
By Jennifer Armstrong

Choose a game or activity to play for 60 minutes as a family or with friends today!

Day 10

Choose a **Play** or **Exercise Activity!**

76

INCENTIVE CONTRACT CALENDAR

My parents and I agree that if I complete this section of

Summer Fit Activities™

and read _____ minutes a day, my reward will be _____

Child Signature: _____   Parent Signature: _____

Day 1	✏️	📖	Day 6	✏️	📖
Day 2	✏️	📖	Day 7	✏️	📖
Day 3	✏️	📖	Day 8	✏️	📖
Day 4	✏️	📖	Day 9	✏️	📖
Day 5	✏️	📖	Day 10	✏️	📖

Color the for each day of activities completed.

Color the for each day of reading completed.

Summer Fitness Log

Choose your exercise activity each day from the Aerobic and Strength Activities in the back of the book. Record the date, stretch, activity and how long you performed your exercise activity below. Fill in how many days you complete your fitness activity on your Incentive Contract Calendars.

	Date	Stretch	Activity	Time
examples:	June 4	Run in place	Sky Reach	7 min
	June 5	Toe Touches	Bottle Curls	15 min
1.				
2.				
3.				
4.				
5.				
6.				
7.				
8.				
9.				
10.				

I promise to do my best for me. I exercise to be healthy and active. I am awesome because I am me.

Child Signature: _____

Decimals can be written as a percent and any percent can be written as a decimal. The decimal 0.43 is read as 43 hundredths, meaning 43 out of 100, which can also be written 43%. 43% also means 43 out of 100, or 43 hundredths, which is 0.43

Change the following percents to decimals and decimals to percents.

1. 52% =

2. 63% =

3. 75% =

4. 17% =

5. 123% =

6. 0.43 =

7. 0.92 =

8. 0.75 =

9. 0.28 =

10. 1.54 =

Milky Way Galaxy

A galaxy is full of stars. Our sun is just one of at least 200 billion stars in the Milky Way galaxy. Our solar system is one of many solar systems, so is our galaxy. Our nearest major neighboring galaxy is called Andromeda. There are believed to be hundreds of billions of galaxies in the Universe.

The Milky Way is spiral shaped, as are other galaxies in the Universe, but some are elliptical and a few look like toothpicks or rings. How do we know what a galaxy looks like when the planet we live on is just a small part of the huge solar system that is one of many in the vast Milky Way galaxy? The Hubble Ultra Deep Field (HUDF) -- a very strong telescope -- can see beyond our galaxy and because it can, we have been able to see what other galaxies look like.

Decide if each statement is true or false.

1. _____ The Milky Way is the only galaxy.

2. _____ Our nearest neighbor galaxy is Andromeda.

3. _____ Our sun is one of at least 20 billion stars in the Milky Way Galaxy.

4. _____ The Milky Way is shaped like a ring.

5. _____ We know more about what is out in space because of the Hubble Telescope.

Pronouns and antecedents

The antecedent is the noun to which a pronoun refers. In the sentence "Mary took her cat to the veterinarian for its checkup," <u>her</u> refers to Mary and <u>its</u> refers to the cat. For the first part of this exercise, circle the word or words to which each pronoun refers. (There may be more than one in a sentence.)

1. Bill and Fred went to their friend's house for dinner.

2. The teacher gave each girl back her paper.

3. The tree grew straight and tall in its pot.

When writing sentences using pronouns, the antecedent must agree with the pronoun in number and gender. This gets a bit confusing with indefinite pronouns, but there are a few rules to help understand this.

1. These indefinite pronouns are singular, and therefore must have a singular antecedent: one, everyone, someone, no one, anyone, everybody, nobody, anybody, somebody, each, either, neither. Most of these have "one" or "body" in the word, and those are singular.

2. These indefinite pronouns are plural and take plural antecedents: several, few, both, many.

3. These indefinite pronouns may be either singular or plural depending on how they are used in a sentence: all, most, any, none. If the sentence has a compound antecedent joined by or or nor, the pronoun agrees with the antecedent closer to it.

Circle the correct antecedent.

4. Each of the girls took (their , her) turn.

5. Neither Bob or Jack brought (their , his) shoes.

6. Most of the kids like (their , his or her) teacher.

7. Somebody should raise (their , his or her) hand.

8. Somebody in the girl's choir lost (their, her) notebook.

9. Either Yvonne or the boys found (their , his or her) ticket to the show.

10. Either the teachers or the principal volunteered (their , his or her) time.

Choose your **STRENGTH** exercise!

Exercise for today:

Check & Record in Fitness Log.

Day 1

Fractions to decimals.

Sometimes a fraction cannot be written with a denominator of 100. You can still write it as a percent by writing the fraction as a decimal. To do this, simply divide the numerator by the denominator.

Example $\frac{5}{8}$ = 5 ÷ 8 = 0.625   To write this as a percent, move the decimal 2 places to the right, giving you 62.5%. Don't go past 3 decimal places when dividing.

1. $\frac{7}{8}$ =

2. $\frac{50}{65}$ =

3. $\frac{26}{40}$ =

4. $\frac{8}{32}$ =

5. $\frac{9}{45}$ =

6. $\frac{17}{34}$ =

American Revolution

People from many countries came to settle in the Americas. In North America, colonies were founded all along the east coast. With the passage of time, Great Britain came to own or administer most of those colonies. For many years, the relationship between Great Britain and the colonies was a comfortable, positive one.

During the 1700s, European scientists and philosophers began to examine the world through reason rather than through religion. This period of time was called the Enlightenment. Some of the great thinkers were Locke, Voltaire, Montesquieu, and Newton. One of the ideas these men promoted was the notion of a social contract between government and the governed.

The American colonists began to feel that this social contract had been violated. They thought that the English government was taxing them unfairly, and not giving them a chance to have a say in the matter. They also felt that the government was using the colonies to supply resources to the mother country. However, from their perspective, the government was giving little or nothing back.

After a series of altercations between the colonists and the British soldiers, officials, and politicians, the colonists decided they should be their own country. They sent representatives to Philadelphia, who drafted a Declaration of Independence, which listed the reasons the colonies felt they deserved to be independent. The Revolutionary War was fought, the colonists won, and a new country was begun.

1. What idea did the Enlightenment thinkers promote which the colonists felt the British government had violated? _____

2. What do we call the list of reasons drafted by the colonial representatives? _____

Characters are the people, animals, and imaginary creatures who take part in a story. The action generally centers around one or two main characters. The other characters in the story are the minor characters. They interact with the main character in order to move the story along.

Characters are revealed in a variety of ways. Often the author gives descriptions of the character. The interaction between the character and others in the story tells a great deal about the individual. Sometimes the author shares the character's thoughts and feelings as well.

Consider this excerpt from *20,000 Leagues Under the Sea* by Jules Verne. The book was published in 1870, when submarines were largely theoretical. Captain Nemo is the commander of a submarine, which he had himself designed and built.

"Ah, commander," I exclaimed with conviction, "your Nautilus is truly a marvelous boat!"

"Yes, professor," Captain Nemo replied with genuine excitement, "and I love it as if it were my own flesh and blood! Aboard a conventional ship, facing the ocean's perils, danger lurks everywhere; on the surface of the sea, your chief sensation is the constant feeling of an underlying chasm, as the Dutchman Jansen so aptly put it; but below the waves aboard the Nautilus, your heart never fails you! There are no structural deformities to worry about, because the double hull of this boat has the rigidity of iron; no rigging to be worn out by rolling and pitching on the waves; no sails for the wind to carry off; no boilers for steam to burst open; no fires to fear, because this submersible is made of sheet iron not wood; no coal to run out of, since electricity is its mechanical force; no collisions to fear, because it navigates the watery deep all by itself; no storms to brave, because just a few meters beneath the waves, it finds absolute tranquility! There, sir. There's the ideal ship! And if it's true that the engineer has more confidence in a craft than the builder, and the builder more than the captain himself, you can understand the utter abandon with which I place my trust in this Nautilus, since I'm its captain, builder, and engineer all in one!"

1. Nemo has been characterized as arrogant. Find evidence in the excerpt which supports this idea. _____

_____

2. Nemo is very proud of his ship. What are two of the things which he says make it ideal?

_____

_____

3. Why did Nemo say they did not have to worry about storms? _____

_____

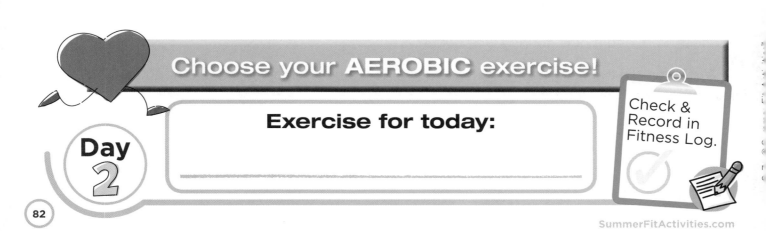

Choose your **AEROBIC** exercise!

Exercise for today:

Check & Record in Fitness Log.

Day 2

Ratio used in scales

You could not draw a diagram of a house on a piece of paper because it is too large. Instead, we use scale, which is a type of ratio. Scale is also used on maps. Many people use scale drawings, such as architects, map makers and engineers. The ratio being used is usually in a legend or key. Use the following diagram and ratio to determine the actual size of the elements of this building. Use the measurement across as wide and top to bottom as long.

	1.5 in	0.5 in	1.25 in
1 in	Kitchen	Bath Room	Bedroom
1 in	Dining Room	Living Room	

Dining Room: 1.5 in
Living Room: 1.75 in

Scale 1 in : 12 ft

1. Kitchen is actually _____ feet wide.

2. Kitchen is _____ feet long.

3. Living Room is _____ feet long.

4. Front of the building is _____ feet wide.

5. Side of building is _____ feet long.

Asteroid Fun Facts

- Asteroids are small bodies made of rock and metal that orbit the Sun.
- Asteroids are similar to comets but do not have a visible coma (fuzzy outline and tail) like comets do.
- Asteroids are also known as planetoids or minor planets.
- Asteroids vary greatly in size, some as small as ten meters in diameter while others stretch out over hundreds of kilometers.
- Objects under ten meters in diameter are generally regarded as meteoroids.
- The first asteroid was discovered in 1801 by Italian astronomer Giuseppe Piazzi.
- The asteroid belt lies roughly between the orbits of Mars and Jupiter in the Solar System.
- It is believed by many scientists and researchers that an asteroid impact was the cause behind the extinction of the dinosaurs around 65 million years ago.

Use at least five of these facts to write a paragraph about asteroids.

_____

_____

_____

_____

_____

_____

Two of the trickiest words in our language are who and whom. At least many people think so.

But here's a simple trick you can use to know when to use each pronoun. Make a question about the sentence. If the answer is he, the pronoun is who. If the answer is him, the pronoun is whom. For the sentence (Who , Whom) wrote the letter?, you would respond **He** wrote the letter. Therefore the correct pronoun is Who. If the sentence is The letter was written to (who , whom)? the answer would be The letter was written to **him**. The correct pronoun is whom.

Circle the correct pronoun for each of these sentences.

1. The children wondered (who , whom) their new teacher would be.

2. The package that came in the mail was addressed to (who , whom)?

3. We want to know on (who , whom) the trick was played.

4. Mrs. Jones consulted a lawyer (who , whom) she met in Indianapolis.

5. (Who , Whom) came to the door to get the pizza?

6. (Who , Whom) are you going to invite?

7. He doesn't know (who , whom) the president of the company is at this time.

8. You may give this award to (whoever , whomever) you please.

9. I can't remember (who , whom) told me that.

10. If I had known (who , whom) she was, I would have visited with her.

11. From (who , whom) have you gotten responses to your request?

12. The three girls (who , whom) were in the store were actually sisters.

13. No one could guess to (who , whom) the letter referred.

14. Do you know to (who , whom) I gave the key to the car?

Choose your **STRENGTH** exercise!

Exercise for today:

Check & Record in Fitness Log.

Day 3

Read a bar graph

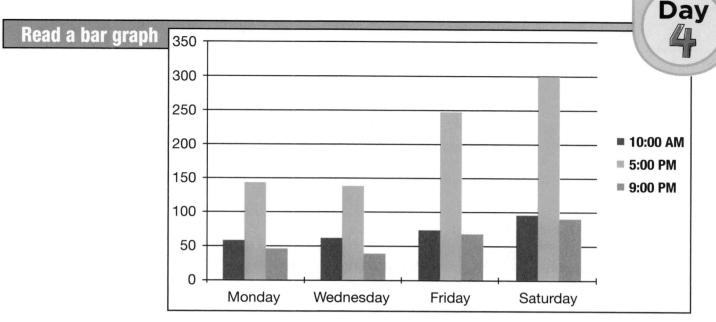

Number of shoppers in the clothing store

1. The store is the busiest at what time each day? _____

2. What is the busiest day and time for the store? _____

3. What reason might that be the busiest day and time? _____

_____

4. What day and time does the store have the least shoppers? _____

French Revolution

Around the time America was fighting for independence, the people of France were becoming discontented. Their society was organized into three groups, called estates. The First Estate was made up of church leaders, the Second Estate was the nobles, and the Third Estate was everyone else (except the king – he didn't belong to any of these groups). The Third Estate included over 95% of the people.

The First and Second Estates enjoyed a life of wealth and comfort. They collected money in the form of taxes and church offerings from the Third Estate, who were already living in poverty. When the Americans declared independence from Britain, some people in France decided to follow their lead and declare "independence" from the king and the upper classes.

The French Revolution was very bloody and violent. By the time it was over, some of the original leaders had been put to death by those who had followed them. The royalty had been overthrown, but the French people felt that the rights due to them as French citizens had been acquired.

1. Which group of people made up the second estate? _____

_____

2. The poor, who were the majority of the people, were in which estate? _____

_____

3. Which estates enjoyed wealth and comfort? _____

_____

A myth is usually a traditional story of events told as if they were history that serves to explore a group of people or explain a practice, belief, or natural phenomenon. Greeks and Romans both wrote myths to explain how they believed their societies began. They also used them to explore character traits in people. In the story of Daedalus and Icarus, Icarus was a typical child who thought his parent was being overprotective.

Most early civilizations created myths. Here is a Native American myth from the Lenape people.

WHEN SQUIRRELS WERE HUGE

Long ago, the squirrel was huge, and walked all over the place, in the valleys, in the woods, and the big forests, looking for smaller creatures to eat. He would eat all kinds of animals, even snakes.

Suddenly one evening he saw a two-legged creature running along. He ran after that two-legged creature, and finally he caught that person, and when he snatched him up he began to tear him to pieces. Finally he ate that person all up except for the person's hand which the giant squirrel was carrying in his hand.

While he was still busy chewing, all at once another person, an enormous person, was standing nearby. That person had a very white light shining and shimmering all around him, and when he said anything he roared like thunder and the earth shook and the trees fell down. He was the Creator.

The Creator said to the squirrel, "Now, truly you have done a very terrible deed. You have killed my child. Now, from this time on it is you who will be little and your children and your great grand-children will be eaten, and the shameful thing you did will always be seen (by a mark) under your forearm." Oh, the squirrel was scared, and he trembled with fear. He wanted to hide the man's hand, and he placed it under his upper arm. This story must be true because for a long time I have cut up and cooked many squirrels, and I have seen the hand under the squirrel's upper arm. We always cut that piece out before cooking the squirrel.

Answer each question **TRUE** or **FALSE**.

1. _____ Early people from many cultures told mythological stories.
2. _____ In the story, originally the squirrel was a very small animal.
3. _____ The person that the squirrel ate was the son of the Creator.
4. _____ The Creator is described as a weak, powerless person.
5. _____ The Creator wanted to reward the squirrel for his bravery.
6. _____ The squirrel wanted to hide the man's hand because it proved he had killed the man.
7. _____ The story suggests that there is a mark under a squirrel's arm which looks like a hand.
8. _____ This story is probably true.

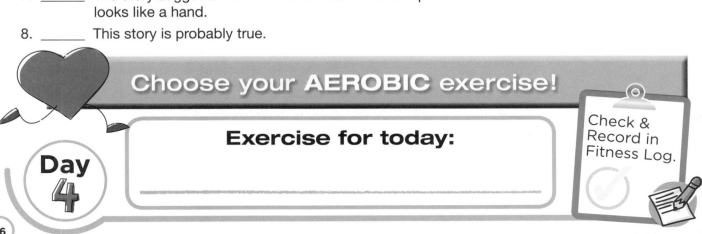

Choose your AEROBIC exercise!

Exercise for today:

Check & Record in Fitness Log.

Day 4

RESPECT

RESPECT – Harry S. Truman

Harry Truman, our 33rd president, grew up in Independence, Missouri. He was a farmer, fought in World War I, and opened a haberdashery (men's clothing store) before becoming active in politics. In 1922, he was elected a judge of the Jackson County Court, where he earned a reputation for honesty and efficiency. He was a senator during World War II, and became Franklin Delano Roosevelt's vice president in 1945. When Roosevelt died, Truman became president.

Truman had respect for the people of the USA. He worked hard to implement programs to help the poor and the elderly. In a 1946 letter to the National Urban League, President Truman wrote that the government has "an obligation to see that the civil rights of every citizen are fully and equally protected." He ended racial segregation in civil service and the armed forces in 1948. For the remainder of his presidency, he continued to fight against segregation.

Value

1. What did Truman do with his life before becoming interested in politics?

_____

_____

_____

2. What qualities did Truman demonstrate as a county judge?

_____

_____

3. What does implement mean?

_____

_____

_____

4. Truman said that government has "an obligation to see that the civil rights of every citizen are fully and equally protected." How did Truman show that he believed this statement?

_____

_____

6-7 • © Summer Fit Activities™

Value:

RESPECT

Respect is showing good manners and acceptance of other people and our planet. Respect is celebrating differences in culture, ideas and experiences that are different than yours. Respect is accepting that others have lessons to teach us because of their experiences.

> "Be the change you want to see in the world."
>
> - Mahatma Gandhi

List 3 ways to show respect to your parents and teachers.

1 _____

2 _____

3 _____

We can disrespect people with our words. Remember to THINK before we speak. Ask yourself...

T = is it true?

H = Is it helpful or hurtful?

I = Is it inspiring?

N = Is it necessary?

K = Is it kind?

WAYS TO SHOW RESPECT

Respect the Earth.
Collect items to recycle.

Respect a different culture:
Listen to some music or try a new food that is associated with a culture or belief that is different than yours.

Day 5

Choose a Play or Exercise Activity!

6-7 • © Summer Fit Activities™

Summer Explorer

Healthy Planet Activities and Fun Things to Do!

- Play flashlight tag in the dark with your family or friends.

- Learn the phases of the moon. Look at it several nights in a row and see if you can recognize the various phases.

- Make cookies and share with someone who could use a sweet treat.

- Start a recycling business in your neighborhood. Promote best ways to separate and recycle.

- Have a water balloon fight with your friends.

- Go to the library and find a fun book to read.

- Learn a new sport or activity — try something you never have tried before.

- Go on a rock collecting walk and collect rocks to paint.

- Make a funny YouTube video.

- Listen to music you do not normally listen to.

- Go on a nature walk. Collect twigs, leaves, pebbles, and shells. Glue them on card stock to make a 3D masterpiece.

- Plant some flowers or a garden.

- Grab some binoculars and go on a bird watching hike.

- Volunteer.

- Organize a backyard Olympics for friends and family.

- Give your pet a bath.

Nature Walk

 Go on a nature walk in a field, park or beach.

 Collect grass, twigs, shells, pebbles, etc.

 Arrange your finds inside a cardboard box, glue down to create a 3D masterpiece.

6-7 © Summer Fit Activities™

Summer Journal IV

Write about your best summer day so far.

Integers

Integers — Whole numbers and their opposites are called integers. Numbers less than zero are called negative numbers (an example is when you owe money). Numbers greater than zero are called positive numbers. Zero is neither positive nor negative. You can compare integers by looking at where they fall on a number line. The greater of two integers is always the one farthest to the right.

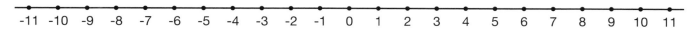

-11 -10 -9 -8 -7 -6 -5 -4 -3 -2 -1 0 1 2 3 4 5 6 7 8 9 10 11

Adding Integers The sum of two positive integers is a positive integer. The sum of two negative integers is a negative integer. To find the sum of a positive integer and a negative integer, you subtract the smaller absolute number from the larger one, then assign the sign of the larger one.

Example 3 + (-5) Think (5 − 3 = 2). 5 is larger than 3 and it's sign is negative, so the answer is -2. You can also use the number line. Begin at 3 and count 5 in the negative direction. You end up at -2.

1. 5 + 9 =

2. 13 + (-6) =

3. 14 + -3 =

4. 7 + (-10) =

5. -7 + (-2) =

6. -5 + 7 =

7. 4 + (-1) =

8. -2 + 0 =

Regions of the US

Region is one of the themes of geography. A region is an area that has something in common. That something could be language, land formations, shared history or culture.

Different sources divide the United States into a different number of geographic regions. We are going to look at 7. There is a long region along the Atlantic and Gulf Coast, called the Coastal Plain. To the west of this and going from northern Georgia and Alabama to Maine is the Appalachian Mountain region. The largest region is call the Interior Lowlands, and reaches from eastern Ohio to Western Missouri and Illinois. The Great Plains is west of that, broken up by the Rocky Mountain region. Along the western coast of the U.S. is the Coastal Range. Between the Coastal Range and Rocky Mountains is the Basin and Ridge region. The division of these regions is based on the basic landforms found in each region.

1. In what region is your home located? _____

2. What landforms are located near your home? (Lakes, mountains, hills, flatland, oceans?)

_____

_____

3. What do you like best about the region in which you live? _____

_____

_____

A sonnet is a particular style of poetry. (The name comes from an Italian word "sonetto" which means little song.) Traditionally, it has 14 lines of iambic pentameter – huh!? That just means that every line has 10 syllables and every other syllable is stressed (soft – LOUD - soft – LOUD - soft – LOUD - soft – LOUD - soft – LOUD).

William Shakespeare, who lived in England in the late 1500s and early 1600s, is considered by many to be the greatest writer in the English language. He wrote about 38 plays, 154 sonnets, two long narrative poems, and several other poems. His sonnets followed a particular rhyme scheme: abab cdcd efef gg.

Sonnet 18 is perhaps the most well known of Shakespeare's sonnets.

Sonnet 18
Shall I compare thee to a summer's day?
Thou art more lovely and more temperate:
Rough winds do shake the darling buds of May,
And summer's lease hath all too short a date:
Sometime too hot the eye of heaven shines,
And often is his gold complexion dimm'd;
And every fair from fair sometime declines,
By chance or nature's changing course untrimm'd;
But thy eternal summer shall not fade
Nor lose possession of that fair thou owest;
Nor shall Death brag thou wander'st in his shade,
When in eternal lines to time thou growest:
   So long as men can breathe or eyes can see,
   So long lives this, and this gives life to thee.

The first line of this poem is very famous and often quoted. The next 11 lines, are the comparison of the person and summer. The last part of the poem tells how the subject is different from summer.

1. Line 2 says the subject is "more lovely and more temperate" than summer. What does temperate mean? _____

2. How does the poet say the summer is not temperate? _____
_____

3. Find the line that suggests that the subject will not seem to grow older. _____
_____

4. There is personification in line 11 – what word is it? _____

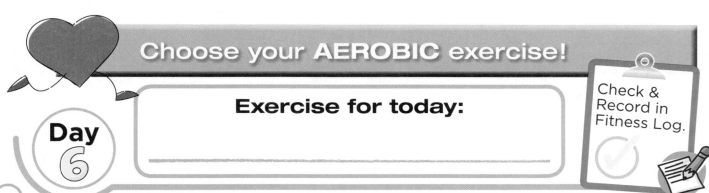

Choose your AEROBIC exercise!

Exercise for today:

Check & Record in Fitness Log.

Day 6

Subtract Integers

To subtract an integer, add it's opposite.

Examples: $3 - 9 = 3 + (-9) = -6$ $-9 - 4 = -9 + (-4) = -13$ $-6 - (-5) = -6 + 5 = -1$

1. $-9 - 12 =$
2. $12 - 37 =$
3. $42 - (-15) =$
4. $-6 - 2 =$
5. $19-17 =$
6. $-19 - 17 =$
7. $-19 - (-17) =$

8. $3 - (-7) =$
9. $-2 - 0 =$
10. $0 - (-7) =$
11. $-13 - (-4) =$
12. $12 - (-9) =$
13. $1 - 0 =$
14. $0 - 1 =$

Observation Game

You will need a partner for this game. You also need 2 sets of 5 to 10 small ordinary objects, such as coins or Legos.   (2 dimes, 2 monopoly houses, etc.)

One person arranges the items from one set on a table. Set a timer for 30 seconds and the second person will study the arrangement on the table. At the end of 30 seconds, cover the objects. The second person now takes the second set of objects and tries to duplicate the arrangement. When finished, check the second arrangement against the first, awarding 1 point for each item the same. Be specific; not only are they in the same order, but for example was the coin heads up or tails, is it turned in the same direction? Use pen and paper to keep track of the score.

Now the second person arranges the objects and the first person tries to duplicate the arrangement. At the end of five rounds, tally the score for each player and crown the champion of observation!

PLAYER ONE :

PLAYER TWO:

6-7 • © Summer Fit Activities™

Playing a musical instrument is a skill that takes time, effort, and a little talent. However, the rewards far outweigh the work that goes into it.

It is quite an accomplishment to learn even the basics of an instrument. You are mastering not only the skill involved in playing. You learn other technical aspects of your instrument: how it is made and put together, and perhaps even how to do simple repairs.

Very often a student learns the history of the instrument. Many instruments date back to pre-historic times. Then there are instruments which have been developed within the last century. A great many instruments are fashioned after previous instruments, but have been altered in some way.

Most instructors will also teach about composers. Some stick to just the more famous composers or time periods. Many prefer to focus on only modern composers. Some like to interject obscure, little known composers who often have composed something of which the teacher is especially fond.

Many people do not realize, however, the connection between music and math! Music in America is written with notes that measure largely in multiples of 2 (whole notes, half, quarter, sixteenths). A piece of music follows a pattern which is set up at the beginning of the piece – which note will get 1 beat in a measure and how many beats are in the measure. The math has to add up. In a measure which is supposed to have 4 beats, you could have a half note, a quarter note and 2 eighth notes. You could not have a half note, 2 quarter notes and an eighth note, because that would equal four and an eighth – too many beats for the measure.

Another way music is tied to math is in the scales we use. Most scales are based on 8 notes. We use the first seven letters of the alphabet to name the notes. Why don't we use the first eight? Because the last note in a scale is a higher version of the first note, and uses the same name.

Who would have thought music could help you with math? In addition, you learn some history, some culture, and a skill which can bring enjoyment to others as well as yourself.

1. Infer from the selection what the word obscure, in the fourth paragraph, means. _____
_____

2. What are two ways music is connected to math? _____
_____

3. What are the technical aspects you might learn with an instrument? _____
_____

4. The selection does not discuss practice, but to do well in anything we have to practice. How often do you think a person should practice a musical instrument. Explain your reasoning.
_____
_____

Choose your STRENGTH exercise!

Exercise for today:

_____

Day 7

Check & Record in Fitness Log.

Multiply and divide integers

The product of two positive or two negative integers is always positive. The product of a positive integer and a negative integer is always negative. Remember that the product of any integer and zero is zero.

1. $-4 \times (-4) =$

2. $-8 \times 3 =$

3. $5 \times (-6) =$

4. $-7 \times (-8) =$

5. $-2 \times 9 =$

6. $5 \times 7 =$

7. $4 \times (-8) =$

8. $-7 \times (-9) =$

The division rule is like the multiplication rule. The quotient of two positive or two negative integers is positive. The quotient of a positive and a negative integer is negative. Zero divided by any other integer is zero. An integer cannot be divided by zero.

9. $54 \div (-9) =$

10. $-63 \div 7 =$

11. $72 \div 8 =$

12. $-36 \div (-6) =$

13. $-30 \div 5 =$

14. $26 \div (-2) =$

15. $-27 \div (-3) =$

16. $-56 \div (-7) =$

World War I

There are two wars that have been labeled as World Wars. They both began in Europe and involved some of the same countries. They are called World Wars because countries from around the world were involved.

World War I began when a Serbian man killed the Austrian heir. The Serbs felt they had been oppressed by the Austrians. The Austrians were allies with Germany. They declared war on Serbia. France and Great Britain declared war on Austria and Germany. Russia also declared war on Austria. Many European countries tried to stay neutral, but several joined one group or the other. America initially refused to take sides, but when Germans continued to attack ships in the Atlantic with Americans, America joined the Triple Entente (Great Britain, France and Russia). The other group was called the Triple Alliance; Italy joined this group.

1. Which countries were part of the Triple Alliance? _____

_____

_____

2. What event sparked the First World War? _____

_____

_____

Soliloquy

One way to think of a soliloquy is that it's a speech you make to yourself. An author may have a character give a soliloquy in order for the reader to understand the character's thoughts and perspective. A more formal definition is a dramatic speech that represents reflections or unspoken thoughts by the character.

The following is a soliloquy by *Alice of Alice In Wonderland*. She has fallen down the rabbit hole after trying to follow the White Rabbit.

ALICE: *[Angrily]* Why, how impolite of him. I asked him a civil question, and he pretended not to hear me. That's not at all nice. *[Calling after him]* I say, Mr. White Rabbit, where are you going? Hmmm. He won't answer me. And I do so want to know what he is late for. I wonder if I might follow him. Why not? There's no rule that I mayn't go where I please. I--I will follow him. Wait for me, Mr. White Rabbit. I'm coming, too! *[Falling]* How curious. I never realized that rabbit holes were so dark . . . and so long . . . and so empty. I believe I have been falling for five minutes, and I still can't see the bottom! Hmph! After such a fall as this, I shall think nothing of tumbling downstairs. How brave they'll all think me at home. Why, I wouldn't say anything about it even if I fell off the top of the house! I wonder how many miles I've fallen by this time. I must be getting somewhere near the center of the earth. I wonder if I shall fall right through the earth! How funny that would be. Oh, I think I see the bottom. Yes, I'm sure I see the bottom. I shall hit the bottom, hit it very hard, and oh, how it will hurt!

1. What is the difference between a soliloquy and a dialogue? _____

_____

2. Why does Alice think a fall downstairs will seem like nothing? _____

_____

3. What does Alice use as her reason for following the rabbit?_____

_____

4. What did Alice say she had not realized before? _____

_____

5. Who does Alice seem concerned about during her fall? _____

6. Why would Alice think she would hit the bottom very hard? _____

_____

_____

Choose your AEROBIC exercise!

Exercise for today:

Check & Record in Fitness Log.

Day 8

Order of Operations

To evaluate mathematical expressions, remember the mnemonic device: **Please Excuse My Dear Aunt Sally**. Work anything in a parenthesis first, then exponents, multiplication and division next, and finally addition and subtraction. Within any of those groupings remember to work from left to right.

Example: -3 x 5 + 2 = -15 + 2 = -13

60 ÷ (5 + 5) = 60 ÷ 10 = 6

---

1. 9 – 6.5 + (-4.1) =

2. -3.5 x -1.4 ÷ 7 =

3. 2 + [48 ÷ (14 + 10)] – 5 =

4. 5 x 9 – [-1.75 x (-3.4)] =

Ocean Water

For this activity you will need a clear bowl, a plastic bottle, table salt, and blue food coloring. Mix ¾ cup of water with 6 tablespoons of salt. Add blue food coloring to make the salty water a deep blue. Fill the bowl half full of water. View the bowl from the side as you pour the blue, salt water down the side of the bowl. Think about what happens when a fresh water river, such as the Mississippi River flows into a salty body of water such as the Gulf of Mexico.

5. Write a paragraph with at least 5 sentences to explain what you think happened in the activity.

_____

_____

_____

_____

_____

_____

_____

_____

_____

An appositive is a noun or a noun phrase that is placed next to another noun or noun phrase to help identify it. If I write, "A student raised his hand," you don't know who that is. If I write, "A student, Hank, raised his hand," then you know that Hank is the student.

Sometimes you need a comma to separate the appositive, sometimes you don't. If the information given by the appositive is essential, you don't use a comma. This would be the case is the sentence doesn't make sense without the appositive. An example is, "The musical group the Beatles wrote a many songs and were very popular in the 1960s." Without the name, the Beatles, the sentence is too vague to make sense.

If the information is not essential, the sentence makes sense without it. Then you set that phrase or noun apart with commas.

Insert an appositive phrase into the first five sentences.

1. I just finished watching my favorite movie, _____.

2. Juan's best friend, _____, went with him to the amusement park.

3. I forgot to feed my pet, a _____.

4. William Shakespeare, an _____ wrote many plays.

5. My school, _____, is a great school.

Decide whether the phrase is an appositive or a prepositional phrase. Mark the appositive sentences with an **A**; mark the prepositional phrases with a **P**.

6. _____ Carolyn played well in the 4th quarter of the match.

7. _____ Abraham Lincoln, the sixteenth president, wrote the Emancipation Proclamation.

8. _____ We'll meet at the park tomorrow.

9. _____ The movie last night, How The West Was Won, was an old one but a great story.

Choose your STRENGTH exercise!

Day 9

Exercise for today:

_____

Check & Record in Fitness Log.

6-7 • © Summer Fit Activities™

RESPONSIBILITY

RESPONSIBILITY – Jimmy Carter

Value

Once a person is no longer president, can they make a difference?

Jimmy Carter, 39th president of the United States, said, "We can choose to alleviate suffering. We can choose to work together for peace. We can make these changes – and we must." Even when we are not responsible for the suffering of others, we must be responsible for helping them whenever and however we can.

To help people follow through on this idea, Jimmy Carter founded the Carter Center. The Carter Center is dedicated to the protection of human rights, disease prevention, conflict resolution and the promotion of democracy.

In addition, Carter and his wife Rosalynn volunteer once a week for Habitat for Humanity. This group takes the responsibility of building and renovating homes for needy people in the United States and other countries. Carter and his wife don't just sit by – they hammer, and clean, and work with everyone else. Jimmy Carter has continued to take responsibility for those in our community who have difficulty helping themselves.

1. What is a habitat? _____

2. What are four things the Carter Center is dedicated to supporting?

1) _____
2) _____
3) _____
4) _____

3. If you were going to help build a home for a needy family, what factors would you look at to determine who deserved the home?

_____
_____
_____

Value: RESPONSIBILITY

You can show responsibility in many different ways. From doing your homework to babysitting your little brother or sister to helping someone else who is in need, being responsible is being accountable for your actions. Big and small, choosing what you do with your time and efforts is an important part of being responsible.

> "I am not doing the run to become rich or famous."
>
> - Terry Fox, *Marathon of Hope*

Monday	
Tuesday	
Wednesday	
Thursday	
Friday	
Saturday	
Sunday	

Build or set up a bird feeder in your yard and be responsible for feeding the birds. Use the chart below to track how many birds you feed for a week.

 We are all responsible for the environment. Watch one of these family movies and talk about how being irresponsible can affect the environment. Movies: *Over the Hedge*, *Hoot*, *Free Willy*, *Bambi*, *Fern Gully*, *The Last Rainforest*, or *Happy Feet*.

Day 10

Choose a Play or Exercise Activity!

6-7 • © Summer Fit Activities™

INCENTIVE CONTRACT CALENDAR

My parents and I agree that if I complete this section of

Summer Fit Activities™

and read _____ minutes a day, my reward will be _____

Child Signature: _____   Parent Signature: _____

Day 1			Day 6		
Day 2			Day 7		
Day 3			Day 8		
Day 4			Day 9		
Day 5			Day 10		

Color the for each day of activities completed.

Color the for each day of reading completed.

Summer Fitness Log

Choose your exercise activity each day from the Aerobic and Strength Activities in the back of the book. Record the date, stretch, activity and how long you performed your exercise activity below. Fill in how many days you complete your fitness activity on your Incentive Contract Calendars.

	Date	Stretch	Activity	Time
examples:	June 4	Run in place	Sky Reach	7 min
	June 5	Toe Touches	Bottle Curls	15 min
1.				
2.				
3.				
4.				
5.				
6.				
7.				
8.				
9.				
10.				

I promise to do my best for me. I exercise to be healthy and active. I am awesome because I am me.

Child Signature: _____

When a ratio compares quantities of different kinds, it is called a rate. The cost of each one of an item is known as the unit rate. The unit rate can be found by dividing the amount of money by the number of items. If a 6 pack of soda costs $4.20, then each soda costs $0.70. Find the unit rate for each of the following.

1. Susan earned $160 for selling 32 boxes of Christmas cards. _____

2. Prime Pizza brought in $656.27 for 73 pizzas. _____

3. The school play seated 1350 people in 30 rows. _____

4. Bill bought 8 tickets for $40. _____

5. Sam collected $325 for 50 books. _____

Scientific Method

Annie designed an experiment for her science class. Read the description and use your knowledge of scientific method to answer the questions.

Many people choose plant experiments for their first project, and so did Annie. She bought a special fertilizer which was advertised to help plants produce more, and larger flowers. She planted two plants of the same size in different containers with the same amount of potting soil. She put one plant in a sunny window and watered it daily with fertilized water. She put the other plant in a shed with no windows behind her house and watered it every other day with plain water.

1. What did Annie do wrong in her experiment? _____

_____

_____

_____

2. What would you do differently to test this product's claims? _____

_____

_____

_____

_____

Alliteration

Alliteration is a device often used in poetry, but also in other literature, in which 2 or more words that are close to each other begin with the same sound. It helps provide a work with musical rhythms and adds interest and appeal. It lends flow and beauty as well as structure to a piece of writing. Poems with alliteration can be easier to memorize.

Alliteration is also used by advertisers to make slogans more memorable. It is also often used with children's stories to make them more fun to read out loud.

Here are some examples of alliteration in Edgar Allen Poe's poem The Raven.

Once upon a midnight dreary while I pondered <u>weak and weary</u>…

And the silken sad uncertain rustling of each purple curtain…

<u>Doubting, dreaming dreams</u> no mortal ever dared to dream before

---

Tongue Twisters are filled with Alliteration. Try saying a few of these tongue twisters three times in a row and quickly.

Peter Piper picked a peck of pickled peppers. A peck of pickled peppers Peter Piper picked. If Peter Piper picked a peck of pickled peppers. How many pickled peppers did Peter Piper pick?

Silly Sally swiftly shooed seven silly sheep. The seven silly sheep Silly Sally shooed shilly-shallied south. These sheep shouldn't sleep in a shack; Sheep should sleep in a shed.

Underline the words in each of the following sentences which demonstrate alliteration.

1. The calico cat caught several fat round mice.
2. The puppies ran round and round the playground.
3. Lovely yellow daffodils and ruby red roses filled the garden.
4. The orchestra performed the opus as beautifully as sweetly singing angels.
5. The sky was full of powder puff clouds.
6. The guitars and drums blended into a rich rhythm of rollicking tunes.
7. As they reached the top of the mountain, their eyes beheld the winter wonder below.
8. Clocks ticked and chimes rang as the boys waited wistfully for the lesson to end.
9. The friendly frog filled the air with his night calls.
10. It seemed that the library was filled with billions of books.

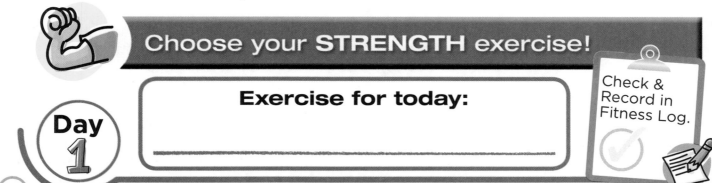

Choose your **STRENGTH** exercise!

Exercise for today:

Check & Record in Fitness Log.

Day 1

1. A 6 oz. can of beans cost $0.69. A 12 oz. can of the same brand costs $1.24.
   What is the best buy, four 6 oz. cans or two 12 oz. cans? What is the difference in cost?

_____

2. You are making a cake and you want to double the recipe. The original recipe calls for
   ¾ cup of sugar, 2 eggs, and 1 and 2/3 cup of flour. How much of each do you need for the
   cake you are making?

Sugar _____   Eggs _____   Flour _____

3. You want to buy 15 "To Go Mugs." How much will it cost if the price is 2 for $0.98? _____

4. You are looking at a diagram of a wall you want to cover with wallpaper. The scale is 1 in = 2
   feet. How tall is the wall if the diagram shows 4 inches? How wide if the diagram shows 6 inches'

Height _____   Width _____

Modern Europe

There are 47 independent countries in Europe. Many people are familiar with the major countries
in Europe, such as Great Britain and France, but not as familiar with some of the smaller countries
(or those not in the news as much.) Find and label these countries on the map.

Albania

Austria

Azerbaijan

Belarus

Bosnia &
Herzegovina

Croatia

Czech Republic

Finland

Greece

Luxembourg

Monaco

Norway

Romania

Serbia

Turkey

Biography

The biography has been a genre of literature popular for hundreds of years. A biography is a story of someone's life, or a portion of that life, written by someone else. Sometimes a biography is written because the author admires the subject, sometimes because the author wants to point out the weaknesses or failings of a person.

An author researches the subject by reading other works about the person, perhaps the subject's diary or journal, and letters or essays written by the subject. The author tries to give the reader more than just basic facts. They try to include personal insights, reflections on the subject's personality, personal information regarding the subject.

Today, biographies are not just books. They may be television programs or movies, online sites, and magazine and newspaper articles.

Remember that biographies are supposed to be factual stories about a person's life. You can tell that a story is a biography if the subject is or was a real person, if the stories are realistic, and usually told in the third person.

Circle the titles or scenarios which would be biographies.

The Cat In the Hat	Pizarro Conquering the Inca
The Story of Thomas Edison's Childhood	Stories of the American Astronauts
George Washington's War Journal	Thomas Jefferson's Diary
George Washington's Journey to Mars	The Presidents' Lives
Peter Rabbit's Amazing Adventures	The Diary of Anne Frank
The Read Adventures of Rabbits	The Wright Brothers and Their Airplane
A story about how horses are trained	A story about the current Queen of England
A story about a queen on the moon	A story about a boy and his dinosaur

Write three sentences about whose biography your might like to read and why.

_____

_____

_____

_____

_____

_____

_____

_____

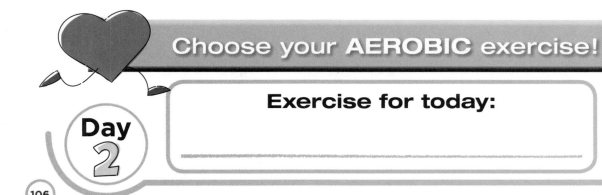

Choose your AEROBIC exercise!

Exercise for today:

_____

Day 2

Check & Record in Fitness Log.

Statistics is the area of math that takes a series of numbers and analyzes them using mean, median, mode, range. The mean is the average – you add the numbers together and divide by how many numbers are in the series. The median is the number that falls exactly in the middle if you put them in order from largest to smallest. If there is no middle number, you take the two in the middle and find the middle of those two. The range is the difference between the greatest and the least number. Mode is a number that appears more often than any other number in the series. (Sometimes there is no mode.) Give the mean, median, mode and range for each set of numbers.

	Mean	Median	Mode	Range
21, 19, 15, 11, 14	16	15	None	10
71, 23, 41, 63, 72				
29, 56, 43, 22, 61, 29				
125, 145, 189, 133				

Scientific Classification

Living things can be divided into 6 kingdoms: Plant, Animal, Protista, Fungi, Archaebacteria, and Eubacteria. Criteria for deciding which kingdom include cell type (complex or single), the ability to make food, and number of cells in the body. Plants, for example, are multicellular and consist of complex cells. They also make their own food. Plants are the second largest kingdom.

The animal kingdom is largest, with over 1 million species. All animals consist of many complex cells. They feed on other organisms.

Archaebacteria are single cell organisms. They are found in extreme environments such as boiling water and thermal vents, with no oxygen or highly acidic conditions. They are complex, as are Eubacteria. Most bacteria are in the Eubacteria kingdom. Most of these are helpful, like those that help produce yogurt and vitamins. Some, however, are not so helpful, such as the ones that cause disease. Some scientists group these two together as simply bacteria.

Mushrooms, mold, and mildew are part of the Fungi kingdom. These are multicellular and have complex cells. They were once thought to be plant cells, but they do not make their own food.

Protista seem to be a catch-all category. This kingdom is all things which are not plants, animals, bacteria, or fungi. Most are unicellular, but have complex cells.

1. Which kingdoms have organisms with single cells? _____

_____

_____

2. Which kingdom would claim as a member the lion? _____

_____

_____

If a direct object is the object of the action of the verb, what is an indirect object? The direct object answers the question "what?" The indirect object answers the question "to whom or for whom?" It is the noun or pronoun that is indirectly affected by the action of a verb.

In the sentence: **Bill played his grandmother a piece on his guitar.** Bill is the subject and played is the verb. He played what? A piece. He played for whom? His grandmother. Therefore, **piece** is the <u>direct</u> object and **grandmother** is the <u>indirect</u> object.

Note that if you use the word "for," as in **He played the guitar for his grandmother**, grandmother is now the object of the preposition for, but is still the indirect object of the sentence.

In the following sentences, circle the indirect object. If there is no indirect object, circle nothing.

1. The mother told the children a bedtime story.

2. Can you bring Julio a glass of water?

3. Claire played the piano beautifully and skillfully.

4. Helene baked the children of the neighborhood some cookies.

5. Dad bought the children each a new bike.

6. Emil gave his sister tickets to the new play.

7. Stewart gave us several options for activities after school.

8. The newspaper was well written.

9. Tell the teacher the reason you are late.

10. Show your dad the story you wrote.

11. Clint scored a goal for the team.

12. Omar sent his sister a postcard from Hawaii.

Choose your STRENGTH exercise!

Exercise for today:

Check & Record in Fitness Log.

Day 3

Comprehension

Mark Twain is probably best known for his books Tom Sawyer and Huck Finn, but he also wrote non-fiction. The following is an excerpt from *Roughing It*, based on events he experienced on a trip with his brother out west.

The next morning, bright and early, we took a hasty breakfast, and hurried to the starting-place. Then an inconvenience presented itself which we had not properly appreciated before, namely, that one cannot make a heavy traveling trunk stand for twenty-five pounds of baggage—because it weighs a good deal more. But that was all we could take—twenty-five pounds each. So we had to snatch our trunks open, and make a selection in a good deal of a hurry. We put our lawful twenty-five pounds apiece all in one valise, and shipped the trunks back to St. Louis again. It was a sad parting, for now we had no swallow-tail coats and white kid gloves to wear at Pawnee receptions in the Rocky Mountains, and no stove-pipe hats nor patent-leather boots, nor anything else necessary to make life calm and peaceful. … I was armed to the teeth with a pitiful little Smith & Wesson's seven-shooter, which carried a ball like a homoeopathic pill, and it took the whole seven to make a dose for an adult. But I thought it was grand. It appeared to me to be a dangerous weapon. It only had one fault—you could not hit anything with it. One of our "conductors" practiced awhile on a cow with it, and as long as she stood still and behaved herself she was safe; but as soon as she went to moving about, and he got to shooting at other things, she came to grief. … Mr. George Bemis was dismally formidable. George Bemis was our fellow-traveler.

We had never seen him before. He wore in his belt an old original "Allen" revolver, such as irreverent people called a "pepper-box." Simply drawing the trigger back, cocked and fired the pistol. As the trigger came back, the hammer would begin to rise and the barrel to turn over, and presently down would drop the hammer, and away would speed the ball. To aim along the turning barrel and hit the thing aimed at was a feat which was probably never done with an "Allen" in the world. But George's was a reliable weapon, nevertheless, because, as one of the stage-drivers afterward said, "If she didn't get what she went after, she would fetch something else." And so she did. She went after a deuce of spades nailed against a tree, once, and fetched a mule standing about thirty yards to the left of it. Bemis did not want the mule; but the owner came out with a double-barreled shotgun and persuaded him to buy it, anyhow. It was a cheerful weapon—the "Allen." Sometimes all its six barrels would go off at once, and then there was no safe place in all the region round about, but behind it.

1. What did Twain mean when he said "the owner came out with a double-barreled shotgun and persuaded him to buy it, anyhow." _____

_____

2. There is a bit of sarcasm in the first paragraph concerning the travelers' clothes. What did Twain infer when he said "we had no swallow-tail coats and white kid gloves to wear at Pawnee receptions in the Rocky Mountains, and no stove-pipe hats nor patent-leather boots." _____

_____

_____

Transitive and Intransitive Verbs

A transitive verb is an action verb that has an object to receive the action. (Remember you can answer the question "what" if there is an object.) Intransitive verbs are action verbs, but there is no object to receive the action. (You might be able to answer where, when, how, or why, but not what.) **In the following sentences, underline the verb and if there is an object, underline that, too. Write a T for the sentences that have a transitive verb, and an I for the sentences with an intransitive verb.**

1. _____ I knitted a blanket.
2. _____ Willow ate until she was stuffed.
3. _____ Candy rode her bicycle around the block several times.
4. _____ My mother baked several pies for Thanksgiving dinner.
5. _____ After the party, Brian moved the chairs back into the dining room.
6. _____ The book fell from my hand onto the floor.
7. _____ Leslie cried all night, and she couldn't seem to stop.
8. _____ I sold some books at the flea market.
9. _____ Ashley broke the window accidentally.
10. _____ The sun rose over the misty mountainside.
11. _____ The committee named a new chairperson during the meeting.
12. _____ The children slept peacefully.
13. _____ Natalia studies Russian in school.
14. _____ Bailey sits in the corner when she reads.

Problem solving

1. Jose is selling online music. His base pay is $5 a day, and he earns an extra $1 for every single song he sells. He wants to earn $100 this week. If he works Monday through Friday, and sells the same number of single songs each day, how many songs does he need to sell each day?

_____

2. If he sells 20 songs on Monday, what is the least he needs to sell the other four days?

_____

3. If he only sells 10 on Monday, what is the least he needs to sell the other four days?

_____

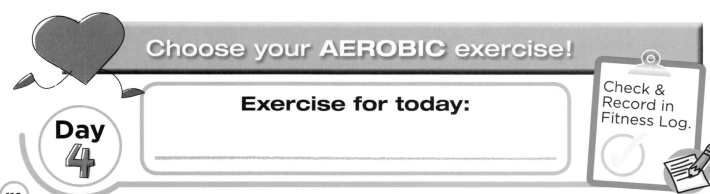

Choose your **AEROBIC** exercise!

Exercise for today:

Check & Record in Fitness Log.

Day 4

PERSEVERANCE

PERSEVERANCE – Wilma Rudolph

Value

Wilma Rudolph was not a healthy child. She had problems with her left leg and for several years had to wear a brace on it. Her family provided physical therapy for her, even though at one time she was told she may not even walk again. But Wilma and her family persevered.

By the time she was in high school, she began to play basketball. She later joined the track team and it was discovered that she was a talented runner. She participated in the 1956 and 1960 Olympics, winning 3 gold medals. Not bad for someone the doctors thought would never walk!

Wilma became a teacher and a coach. Her story was made into a television film and she was inducted into the U. S. Olympic Hall of Fame. She established the Wilma Rudolph Foundation to promote amateur athletics.

1. Who thought Wilma would possibly not walk after her leg problems? _____

_____

_____

2. What sports did Wilma participate in during high school? _____

_____

_____

3. What does the word amateur mean? _____

_____

_____

4. Number these events in the correct order from the story.

_____   Wilma was inducted into the U. S. Olympic Hall of Fame.

_____   Wilma won 3 Olympic gold medals.

_____   Wilma established a foundation to promote amateur athletics.

_____   Wilma was told she might not walk again.

_____   Wilma participated in basketball and track during high school.

_____   Wilma became a teacher and a coach.

Value: PERSEVERANCE

FAMILY ACTIVITIES

Choose one or more activities to do with your family or friends.

 As a family, tackle a big job you have been putting off such as cleaning the garage or painting the fence. Work together as a family to persevere and finish the job. Celebrate with ice cream to emphasize the sweet satisfaction of a job well done.

 People with disabilities face many obstacles each day. Read about Helen Keller and her perseverance in overcoming her blindness and deafness. Put on a blindfold and imagine how hard it would be to go about your day without your sight. What can you do? What can't you do?

 Farmers need perseverance and a lot of patience when planting their crops. One bad storm or drought can destroy everything they have worked for. Plant a small vegetable garden and take care of weeding and watering it. Be patient and your perseverance will pay off.

Let's talk about it...

Talk with your child about what perseverance is and why it's important. Discuss the importance of not giving up and sticking with something until it is complete. Lead by example and point out something you are involved in that is difficult and share with he/she how and why you are going to finish.

VALUES ARE A FAMILY AFFAIR

Read more about PERSEVERANCE

Fly, Eagle, Fly
By Desmond Tutu

I Knew You Could
By Wally Piper

Strawberry Girl
By Lois Lenski

Choose a game or activity to play for 60 minutes as a family or with friends today!

Day 5
Choose a **Play** or **Exercise** Activity!

112

Summer Explorer

Healthy Planet Activities and Fun Things to Do!

- Read a book based on a movie you have seen.

- Make fresh lemonade.

- Go to the park and play on the playground — take a younger brother or sister.

- Spend the day at the library, explore all the different things there to do.

- Write a letter and mail it.

- Volunteer at a local animal shelter.

- Email a friend or relative you have not talked with for a while.

- Camp in the backyard.

- Pretend you are a reporter. Interview someone in your neighborhood and write an article about him/her.

- Make a homemade pizza.

- Plan a picnic for your family or friends.

- Learn a new board or card game.

- Create a music playlist for a friend.

- Make a telescope out of paper towel tubes. Have a family stargazing night: How many constellations can you find? Can you find the Big Dipper? Polaris?

- Create a new smoothie, share it with your family.

- Do some nature drawings.

- Help a neighbor weed their garden.

- Create a theme and make a collage out of old nature magazines.

Stargazing

 Collect paper towel tubes.

 Gather your family on a clear night to stargaze through your "telescopes".

 Look for The Big Dipper, Cancer and other star constellations.

Summer Journal V

Write about your favorite pet or animal.

Autobiography

An autobiography is the story of a person's life or events in someone's life written by that person. Journals and diaries are considered autobiographical. Memoirs are also autobiographical. Jack London wrote a book called *The Road* with stories about his days as a hobo. Benjamin Franklin, Frederick Douglass, and Helen Keller all wrote about their own lives. Anne Frank wrote a diary which was published after her death. All of these stories are told by the individuals about themselves.

Autobiographies are usually written in the first person (I, me, we). The advantage over a biography is that you are privy to the subjects most intimate thoughts. The disadvantage is that people are sometimes less than frank about themselves, especially if there are things they are ashamed of or embarrassed about.

Read this short autobiography to find out about a girl named Veronica.

I loved belonging to a large family. I was the second child and the first daughter. Of the thirteen children, only two were boys: Curtis was the oldest and Paul was the fourth child. After me, as far as the girls, came Edie, Steffie, Jennie, Theresa, Cece, Liz, Sheila, Celeste, Miriam, and Tish.

People always express their sympathy for the boys, but I don't think they deserve any sympathy. Curtis was a great older brother, but he was very manipulative, as well. He was able to work the rest of us. I mean, on Halloween, he would get people to trade him one of something they had for two of something he had. But somehow, he ended up with the best stuff. We had more, but it wasn't as good. To this day, I dislike the game Monopoly, because you couldn't beat Curtis. Again, he would talk you into deals that seemed great, but in the end they benefitted him the most.

Paul probably had it a little tougher. By the time he got to high school, our father had left, and Curtis was entering the military. Paul had to deal with a bunch of teen-age sisters, and a mother, with no adult males in the picture. I like to think we helped him find and develop his feminine side, because he has matured into a thoughtful, loving husband.

Now, don't think we girls were always loving and sweet to each other. We had our spats, for sure. I'm a grown woman, now, but I still remember being so angry when one of the girls "borrowed" without my knowledge my favorite skirt, and when I got it back it had a terrible ink stain that would never come out. For the most part, though, we looked out for one another, helped one another, and we always loved one another.

1. Why did the oldest brother not deserve sympathy?_____

_____

2. How did Paul benefit from having so many sisters? _____

_____

3. What might be a disadvantage of being from a large family? _____

_____

4. What might be an advantage? _____

_____

Probability

Probability is a measure of how likely an event is. For example, if you have a spinner with 6 numbers on 6 equal spaces, the likelihood of landing on any one number is 1 in 6. In other words, you have 1 out of 6 chances of landing on any number. If the numbers are 1 through 6, you have a 3 in 6 chance of landing on an odd number. This probability can be written as a fraction and can be simplified to 1/2 or 1 in 2 chance.

A glass jar contains 6 red, 5 green, 9 blue and 4 yellow marbles.

1. If a single marble is chosen at random from the jar, what is the probability of choosing a red marble? _____

2. What is the probability of choosing a green marble? _____

3. What is the probability of choosing a blue marble? _____

4. What is the probability of choosing a yellow marble? _____

Modern Africa

Africa is the second largest continent in the world. It is three times the size of the continental United States.

There are five huge river systems in Africa. The three biggest are the Nile, the Congo, and the Niger. The other two large river systems are the Orange and the Zambezi. Early civilizations developed along these rivers. One of the most well known is the civilization of Ancient Egypt. Rivers and lakes are still a major source of transportation and communication. They provide food in the form of fish. Fresh water is important for irrigation and for animals. Rivers also provide a very important source of power, hydro-generated electricity. Areas of dense population are centered along rivers and river basins.

Africa has rainforests, grasslands, and is home to the largest desert in the world, the Sahara. Africa does have a few mountain ranges, like the Atlas Mountains in the north. These are fairly large mountains, but they would seem small next to the Alps or the Himalayas. There are no huge mountain ranges in Africa.

1. Africa is the _____ largest continent in the world.

2. You could put the United States in Africa _____ times.

3. The three biggest river systems in Africa are the _____, the _____, and the _____.

4. Africa does not have any large _____.

Choose your **AEROBIC** exercise!

Exercise for today:

Check & Record in Fitness Log.

Day 6

Percent

There are many situations where it is appropriate to tip a person for the service they have given (in addition to the product you have purchased). People who wait tables in restaurants count on tips to supplement their base pay, so do hairdressers, newspaper carriers and cab drivers. Most people tip 10%, 15%, or 20%, depending on how good they thought the service was. An easy way to determine a tip is to begin with 10%, which is easy to figure. You simply take the amount being charged and move the decimal point one position to the left. So for a $45.23 bill at a restaurant, 10% would be $4.52. 20% is twice that amount, in this case $9.02. 15% would be 10% plus half of that. In our example, $4.52 plus $2.26, for a total of $6.78. **Figure the three percentages for each of the following amounts.**

1. $23.75   10% _____   15% _____   20% _____

2. $78.41   10% _____   15% _____   20% _____

3. $54.66   10% _____   15% _____   20% _____

Erosion

Erosion is the process that breaks things down. Rain and wind break down the earth and move the land. If an event occurs with strong rain or wind, you may see the effects of erosion very soon after. Most erosion, however, takes many years to effect a change.

As they age, mountains are worn down by weathering, mass wasting and erosion. Weathering takes place as rocks are broken down into smaller and smaller pieces due to the effects of weather. They do not move to another location, they just break down where they are. As water freezes and thaws, it breaks down rocks. Weathering can also be caused by chemical reactions.

Biotic weathering is caused by living organisms. A plant can grow through a split in a rock and make it worse. Animals digging is another form of biotic weathering.

The most common mass wasting is falling. Rocks, boulders, and dirt loosened by wind, rain, or freezing, simply fall downward.

Erosion takes place when materials move from one location to another. This happens when dust is blown down the side of the road or silt is washed down a river.

Unscramble the words by looking for them in the section above.

1. grehaeiwtn _____

2. osreoin _____

3. twiansg _____

4. coibti _____

5. hicalemc _____

Theme is the meaning or moral of a story. It is often a message about life or human nature that the author shares with the reader. It is different from the subject of a story – that is what a particular story is about, its characters, the important events. Theme is the meaning behind the story. Sometimes a theme is stated directly, as in some folktales and fables. Often, though, the author wants you to figure out the theme by paying attention to what is said and what happens in the story.

A typical theme might be that family is more important than anyone else, or honesty is an important trait to develop. **Lets look at the folktale "Stone Soup" to find the theme.**

A soldier was on his way home from the war. As he passed through a small village, close to nightfall, he realized he was very hungry. He stopped at a cottage and asked the woman there if she had any food to share with him. She was very wary of this stranger and so she yelled that she had no food and to go away!

The soldier moved away from the woman's house, but he didn't go away. He stood thinking for a minute, then he took from his pack a fairly large pot. He looked around and found an area near the road where he could build a fire. He filled his pot with some water from the nearby stream, and set it on the fire to heat. When he was sure the woman was looking out her window, he placed three very large stones in the pot.

The woman was very curious about this, so she shouted out the window and asked what he was doing? He replied that he was making stone soup. He said surely she had heard of stone soup before as it was a great delicacy in the homes of many rich people. She said she had not heard of it before, but was very curious.

He went on to say that of course, it would be better if he had a few vegetables: some corn, potatoes, perhaps a few carrots. She said that she had some of those and she would be glad to share if she could have some of the soup when he finished. And he told her that absolutely she could share, though it would be even better if they had a bit of meat in it. She excitedly said that she did have some meat they could put in. As he stirred all the ingredients in, he mentioned that a bit of salt and pepper would just about make it perfect, and wouldn't some biscuits and butter go nicely? The woman ran to the house to fetch the things he suggested.

Finally, the soup was ready, and the soldier and the woman had a fine feast. The soldier kindly let the woman keep the leftover soup, and she declared it was the best she had ever had.

1. What did the soldier trick the woman into doing? _____

2. What would you think is the theme of this story?_____

3. What did the soldier say to make the woman want to try the soup? _____

4. What is a delicacy? _____

Choose your STRENGTH exercise!

Day 7

Exercise for today:

_____

Check & Record in Fitness Log.

Simple percent

Many teachers use simple percents to figure out your grades. They take an average of the scores you have earned and convert the number into a percent. Some teachers also weight grades. In other words, different categories are worth a different percent of your grade. They take the average of your tests, for instance, and count them as 35% of the final grade. Homework may be worth 20%, class work another 20% and quizzes the final 25%.
Use the chart below to help you figure out some possible grades.

	Tests x 35%	Quizzes x 25%	Homework x 20%	Class work x 20%	Total
Example	31.15	19.5	19	18.2	91.41
Francisco					
Emily					

Example: Test average 89, Quiz average 78, Homework average 95, Class work average 91
Francisco: Tests 76, Quizzes 79, Homework 95, Class work 90
Emily: Tests 92, Quizzes 89, Homework 71, Class work 85

South America

South America is the fourth largest continent and is located mostly in the Southern and Western Hemispheres. The Atlantic Ocean washes the Eastern Shore and the Pacific, the Western Shore. The second longest river in the world, the Amazon, runs through South America, as well as the Andes Mountains.

Spain and Portugal colonized most of South America, so Spanish and Portuguese are the most common languages spoken.

The world's largest tropical rain forest covers more than half of Brazil and runs through several other South American countries – The Amazon Rain Forest. Scientists think that about half of the world's species live in the rain forest. It is one of the last safe places for some animals, such as pink dolphins and jaguars. 40,000 plant species, 3,000 freshwater fish species and more than 370 reptile species exist in the Amazon.

Many people are concerned because of the deforestation that is taking place in the Amazon forest. People native to the forest are being displaced, as are many of the animal and plant species. Scientist fear that the deforestation will cause environmental problems because forests and rainforests absorb large quantities of CO_2 (carbon dioxide). CO_2 is harmful greenhouse gas mostly responsible for global warming and climate change. Many people fear that without rainforests a lot more of this gas will end up in the atmosphere causing global warming to be more severe.

1. Why are people concerned about the deforestation of the Amazon Rain Forest? _____

_____

_____

_____

Identifying a dependent clause

A dependent clause is a group of words that has both a subject and a verb, but cannot stand alone as a sentence. An example is: **Wherever she goes, trouble follows her**. Wherever she goes makes no sense without the rest of the sentence – it is incomplete. Another example is: **The only one of the seven dwarves who does not have a beard is Dopey**. Who does not have a beard is the dependent clause – because it is incomplete.

Underline the dependent clause in each of the sentences.

1. That is the ball that I was bouncing.
2. If at first you don't succeed, try something else.
3. Where is the package that I ordered?
4. Many people don't know who their state representative is.
5. I will fix some dinner when I get home.
6. Many planes fly over the city.
7. Even though he is angry, he is being polite.
8. Because I was late, I missed most of the movie.
9. Although I found the library book, I still owed a fine.
10. The crew had seen the whale, which was following the boat.
11. Since I have a large garden, it's helpful that I enjoy weeding.
12. Once Steven smashed the spider, Amy calmed down.
13. Even though it was dark, the children loved playing outside.
14. Grandma decided to put her garden behind the house where the land was level.

Simple Percent

Everyone likes to buy things on sale. Sale prices are usually calculated by using percent. If a shirt is usually $29.95, and the sale price is 20% off, the shirt is now $23.96 ($29.95 minus $5.99, which is 20%). Sometimes the item is already marked down a certain percent, and you have a coupon for another percentage off – then you really save!!

For each question, tell the amount saved and the final price

1. Original price $34.20, sale 15% off _____ _____

2. Original price $42.50, sale 9% off _____ _____

3. Original price $27.65, sale 25% off _____ _____

4. Original price $36.75, sale 15% off, additional coupon 10% _____ _____

Choose your **AEROBIC** exercise!

Exercise for today:

Check & Record in Fitness Log.

Day 8

Mood is the feeling the writer tries to create for the reader. The setting can affect the mood dramatically. A story that takes place during the London Olympics of 2012 will have a different mood from a story that takes place in the jungles of India.

Tone implies the writer's attitude toward the subject. A writer may use humor to write about a subject not thought to be serious, but a serious tone toward a subject thought to be important.

Highwaymen were robbers of the 17th and 18th centuries. They would stop the carriages of the upper classes. They were glamorized in song and story by the poor, who somehow felt avenged against the rich by the actions of the highwaymen. *The Highwayman* by Alfred Noyes tells one of these stories. Here are some excepts from that poem.

Verse One

The wind was a torrent of darkness among the gusty trees.
The moon was a ghostly galleon tossed upon cloudy seas.
The road was a ribbon of moonlight over the purple moor,
And the highwayman came riding – Riding – riding –
The highwayman came riding, up to the old inn-door.

Verse Five

"One kiss, my bonny sweetheart, I'm after a prize tonight,
But I shall be back with the yellow gold before the morning light;
Yet, if they press me sharply, and harry me through the day,
Then look for me by moonlight, Watch for me by moonlight,
I'll come to thee by moonlight, though hell should bar the way."

Verse 8

They said no word to the landlord. They drank his ale instead.
But they gagged his daughter, and bound her, to the foot of her narrow bed.
Two of them knelt at her casement, with muskets at their side!
There was death at every window; And hell at one dark window;
For Bess could see, through her casement, the road that he would ride.

True or False

1. _____ The first stanza sets a pleasant relaxed mood for the poem.

2. _____ The words "riding – Riding – riding" give a sense of urgency to the poem, as

   if the rider is hurrying to the inn.

3. _____ The second verse implies that the highwayman loves the woman.

4. _____ The words "death at every window" change the mood to one of danger.

5. _____ The tone suggests that the author really dislikes the highwayman's character.

There are 8 independent countries in Central America. Find and label these countries on the map.

1. Belize

2. Costa Rica

3. El Salvador

4. Guatemala

5. Honduras

6. Mexico

7. Nicaragua

8. Panama

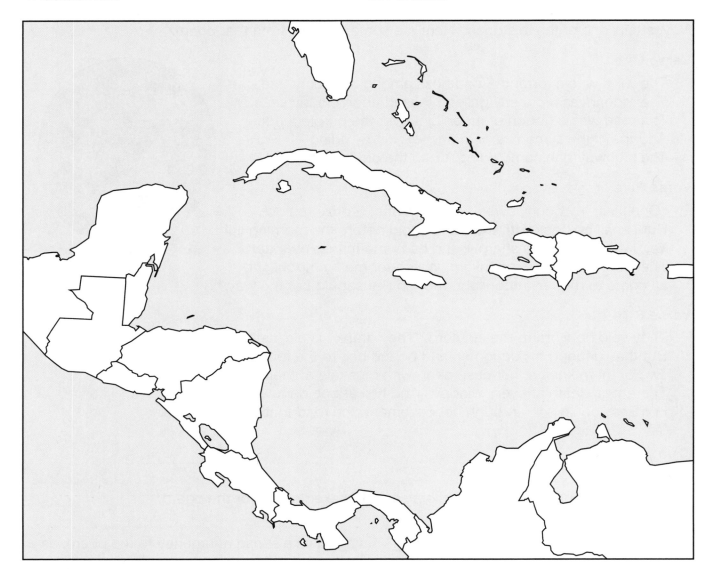

  Choose your **STRENGTH** exercise!

Day 9

Exercise for today:

_____

 Check & Record in Fitness Log.

FRIENDSHIP

FRIENDSHIP – Helen Keller and Anne Sullivan

Value

Helen was less than two years old when an illness left her deaf and blind. Her family did not know how to help her, and as a result, she became an undisciplined and unruly child. Just prior to her 7th birthday, Anne Sullivan came to live with the Keller family, and changed Helen's life as well as her own.

Anne was only 20 years old and her own vision was severely impaired. She had lived a difficult childhood as a ward of the state of Massachusetts. She felt that obedience, patience, and love were the key to reaching Helen. In her biography, Helen wrote, "The most important day I remember in all my life is the one on which my teacher, Anne Mansfield Sullivan, came to me."

Anne stayed with Helen for most of the rest of their lives. She became more than a teacher – she was a mentor and a friend. Anne accompanied Helen when she traveled for pleasure and on lecture tours. When Anne married John Macy, she and her husband continued to live with Helen, until the Macys separated.

Anne and Helen lived and traveled together until Anne's death in 1926. When Helen died, her ashes were buried next to Anne.

1. Anne showed friendship for Anne by living with her and traveling with her. How do you

   show friendship to your friends? _____

   _____

   _____

2. What problem did Anne and Helen share? _____

   _____

3. How can sharing a difficulty lead to friendship? _____

   _____

   _____

4. What qualities did Anne think would help her to reach Helen? _____

   _____

   _____

Value:

FRIENDSHIP

"Don't walk behind me; I may not lead. Don't walk in front of me; I may not follow. Just walk beside me and be my friend."

– Winnie the Pooh

```
H O N E S T W S Q M M H B E T O H L
P K K P K H U C V C Z S E R U D R U
G D X D O O C P P B H N U F E M S F
W A K W R Y R F I A G D V A Z D Q T
F U V E L O P D N J I V C A O S Y C
E G N M K L Y U O K L P E K W J R E
Y E L K K L I E H H O Q H H O O T P
G I J I K T D S U T Y Z Z C T M W S
E K N B A P Y K T J A M R D O Z B E
N D C U W T P X U E L L P W B G K R
Z R Y B W L M B K S N N R Q Z D B H
X R G G U F Q J S R P P S T K I M V
G W V C U K B D R Z W N N V G T A B
U P G J G K L D G X U T H B R I C I
Y I A F Q S X S U I B P R L L H E P
K N I P F B J Y D M R K U O J T Q P
```

Find the words below that are qualities of a good friend.

WORD BANK

fun	listen
loyal	generous
honest	respectful
kind	

Be a Good Friend

 Invite a friend over. Let them choose what to play first.

 Watch *Toy Story* with your family. Talk about how the characters in the movie portray true friendship.

 Make a friendship bracelet for one of your friends. Give it to them and tell them why you are happy to be friends.

 **Day 10**

Choose a Play or Exercise Activity!

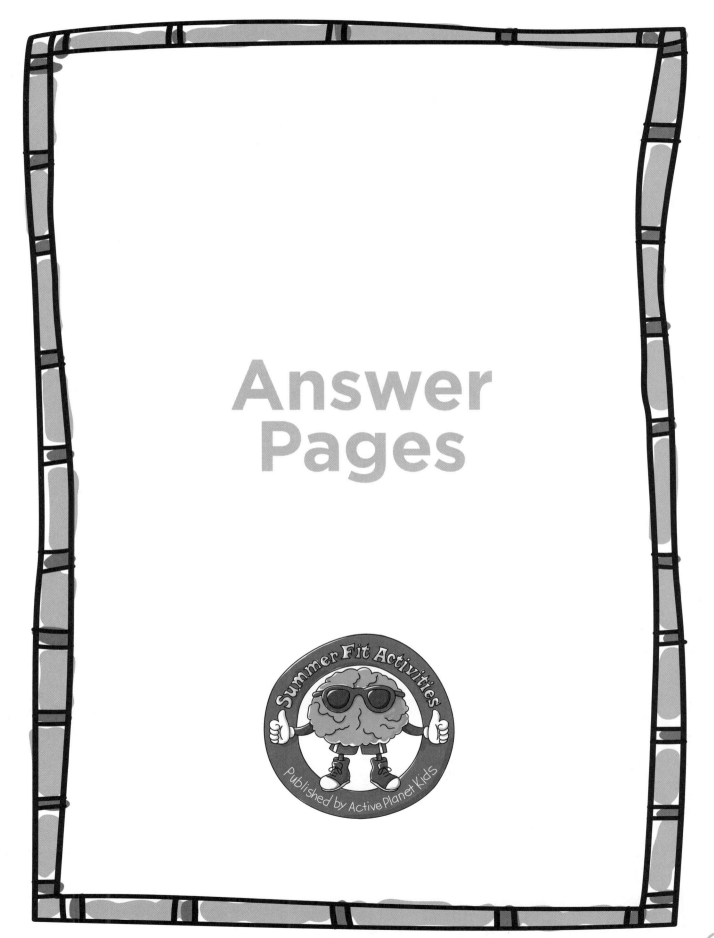

Answer
Pages

Answer Key

P. 1-4 — Summer Skills Review

Math Answers:

1. 18,219 2. 4.7 3. 707
4. 14,858 5. 2,254 6. 739.52
7. 54.914 8. 17,208 9. 104,856
10. 34,773 11. 155.8 2. 340.3
13. 1769.16 14. 791.7 15. 18,25
16. 3874.86 17. 87 18. 71
19. 4.25 20. 37 21. 5.41
22. 52.3 23. 6 24. 30
25. 3/12 and 1/4
26. a. 5/6 b. 4/15 c. 3/4
27. 16/3
28. a. 3/5 b. 1 3/8 c. 10 13/15
29. a. 3/5 b. 2/15 c. 5 8/15
30. 8/15 31. 12 3/5 32. 6
33. 7 34. n = 12 35. a = 15
36. 67% 37. ? = 5 38. 43%

Reading Answers:

1. c 2. a 3. d 4. b
5. g 6. f 7. h 8. e
1. c 2. a 3. e 4. a
5. d 6. d 7. a 8. b
9. e 10. c 11. b 12. c
13. a 14. e 15. d 16. d
17. e 18. b 19. a 20. c
1. b 2. a horn in her forehead 3. c
4. cold, white (which is probably snow)

p. 7 — Day 1:

1. nucleus
2. Nuclear envelope, centriole,
1. 18, 225 2. 22,263 3. 24, 508
4. 33,160 5. 27,196 6. 14,310
7. 23,281 8. 20,000

Correct work every day or two to help keep students accountable. This also shows your child you are interested in their work.

p. 8 — Day 1:

Honesty, Charm, Integrity, Bravery, Courage, Humor, Kindness, Charity, Fear, Hope, Anger, Talent, Innocence, Confidence, Manners

p. 9 — Day 2:

Cities circled on the map – check a map or a globe

1. 0.97 2. 30.52 3. 24.24
4. 38.99 5. 72.86 6. 69.01
7. 2.885 8. 38.596 9. 28.901
10. 366.906

p. 10 — Day 2:

1. agree 2. wants 3. like
4. were 5. seem 6. is
7. were 8. appeal 9. doesn't
10. don't 11. plays 12. clap
13. was 14. bark 15. hangs
1. 642 2. 246 3. 81
4. 287 5. 6,061 6. 1,381
7. 7,811 8. 6,151

p. 11 — Day 3:

1. Jo doesn't want to act like a lady. Answers will vary – need two supporting claims
2. She puts her hands in her pockets, and she whistles.

p. 12 — Day 3:

1. animal 2. Plant 3. Plant
4. Any 2 differences

p. 13 — Day 4:

1. learned the father's trade
2. run a house
3. Answers will vary, but should reflect what was in the section
1. 6.12 2. 22.27 3. 57.944
4. 257.81 5. 41.03
6. 241.44 7. 19.64
1. 37,632 2. 18,837 3. 29,000
4. 295,488 5. 446,490
6. 239,571 7. 53,884

p. 14 — Day 4:

1. her 2. I, she 3. I, he
4. They 5. I, he 6. We
7. he, them 8. he, I, him
9. They, me, them 10. him, her
11. He, I 12. I 13. We, they
14. me 15. them, us

p. 15 — Day 5:

1. Islamabad 2. Answers will vary
3. He could have found many uses for the money for himself and his family.
4. An award for honesty

p. 19 — Day 6:

Summary paragraph of a book

p. 20 — Day 6:

1. 34.5 2. 585.6 3. 391.5
4. 73.1 5. 98 (98.0) 6. 461.5
7. 464.8 8. 451.2 9. 30
10. 480 11. 77.7 12. 480
1. Mild, pleasant climate
2. Answers will vary – might include chairs, floor mats, tables

p. 21 — Day 7:

"heat energy moves between the two objects"

1. 1432.56 2. 1449.89 3. 1005.29
4. 964.44 5. 3409.02 6. 777.36
7. 3843.56 8. 549.43

p. 22 — Day 7:

1. trash – but 2. my – oh
3. ask – or 4. charger – all
5. important – are 6. dinner – flour
7. us – Alice and me – to
8. Callie – my calico cat – to
9. party – music
10. park – oh

p. 23 — Day 8:

Car, Mannequin, Radio, Mailbox

1. 99 2. 137
3. 249 4. 91.16 or 91 R 1
5. 55.44 or 55 R 4 6. 150.8

p. 24 — Day 8:

Sentences: 2-5-6-8-9-11-12-15: Should be circled.

1. 0.121 2. 25.1 3. 56.3
4. 83.1 5. 5.23

p. 25 — Day 9:

1. I'm very hungry.
2. I have a lot of things to do.
3. I had a lot of homework.
4. I'll be upset if I can't buy that dress.
5. He's very thin.
6. This car is very fast.
7. The car is very expensive.
8. That is a very old joke.
9. He's very rich.
10 . I was really surprised
11. I've told you many times.
12. He's very old.
Answers will vary – should describe what was observed during the activity

Answer Key

p. 26 — Day 9:
1. for the British
2. not human
3. below standard
4. spell wrong
5. not inflammatory
6. more than human
7. not regular
8. across the Atlantic
9. not correct
10. written after

p. 27 — Day 10:
1. Not taking proper care of someone or something
2. To make a difference in someone's life, often leading them in a particular direction
3. South Africa
4. Answers will vary

p. 31 — Day 1:
1. Troposphere   2. Exosphere
3. Stratosphere   4. Thermosphere
5. Mesosphere
1. 284   2. 23   3. 1.81
4. 83.5   5. 91.6

p. 32 — Day 1:
1-3. Answers will vary

p. 33 — Day 2:
1. 5   2. 12   3. 3   4. 3
Paragraph with three reasons

p. 34 — Day 2:
1. Answers will vary – may reflect that the lion is considered kingly and Sundiata was considered a good king.
2. Answers will vary.
1. tool to use with the computer, small rodent
2. Vacation, fall
3. Time of year, flavoring for food
4. in attendance, a gift
5. amount of time, coming after first

p. 35 — Day 3:
1. 14(3-1)   2. 18(2-1)   3. 12(1+3)
4. 3(5+6)   5. 3(7-6)   6. 2(22-6)
7. 6(7-2)   8. 3(7+6)   9. 12(3-2)
10. 15(3-2) 11. 21(1+2) 12. 9(4-3)
1. Amused the lion to think the mouse could help
2. Mouse chewed through the net
3. Hunters thought the lion could not escape because he was unable to move
4. Answers will vary

p. 36 — Day 3:
Answers will vary
1. clean, clear, neat (may vary)
2. sharp, pungent, biting (may vary)
3. car, coach, transport (may vary)
4. ruthless, unmercial, relentless (answers vary)
5. expect, foresee, await (may vary)

p. 37 Day 4:
1. 6, 9, 12, 15, 18
2. 8, 12, 16, 20, 24
3. 10, 15, 20, 25, 30
4. 12, 18, 24, 30, 36
5. 14, 21, 28, 35, 42
6. 16, 24, 32, 40, 48
7. 18, 27, 36, 45, 54
8. 10   9. 24   10. 30   11. 18
1. Answers will vary
2. Answers will vary
3. Any 3: protection, transportation, water for cooking and drinking, fishing, washing, enjoyment

p. 38 — Day 4:
1. c   2. e   3. a   4. b
5. d   6. c   7. a   8. d
9. b   10. e   11. b   12. a
13. d   14. e   15. c
1. 1/3   2. 7   3. 25   4. 1

p. 39 Day 5:
1. Any four of the following: Truman, Eisenhower, Nixon, Kennedy, Johnson, Reagan
2. Not fully believing something or someone
3. Cronkite researched his information carefully, and was careful in how he presented his stories. His facts were correct.
4. President Jimmy Carter

p. 43 —Day 6:
Circle sets 1, 4, 6, and 7
Answers will vary

p. 44 — Day 6:
1. station   2. lying   3. curtain
4. butcher   5. daughter   6. surprise
7. complaint 8. passengers   9. lining
10. whisper   11. rhythm   12. divine
13. fulfill   14. kindergarten
15. attendance
1. >   2. <   3. <
4. >   5. <   6. >

p. 45 — Day 7:
1. ababcdcd   2. abcb   3. abcbdd

p. 46 — Day 7:
1. I   2. C   3. I   4. I
5. I   6. C   7. C   8. C
9. I   10. I   11. I   12. I
13. C   14. C
1. Full moon
2. New moon
3. Waxing crescent
4. Waxing Gibbous
5. Waning crescent
6. Waning Gibbous

p. 47 — Day 8:
1. They made farmland by building floating gardens.
2. It was a good site
3. Answers will vary
1. identical   2. very big
3. black   4. blind
5. sink and whistle
6. Mark and ice
7. Claire and the fox
8. Pierre and the peacock

p. 48 — Day 8:
1, 4, 5, 6, 9, 10
1. 2/3   2. 1/3   3. 1/3
4. 2/5   5. 1/4   6. 1/2
7. 1/5   8. 2/3   9. 5/8
10. 1/4

Reward well done and completed work with stickers, stamps or hand written messages.

#1

Answer Key

1. The earth   2. Northern winter
3. The moon is moving around the earth

1. His grandfather saves things just like a pack rat does.
2. The man has an explosive temper.
3. Eyes light things up.
4. He is low like a worm.
5. Schools are like farmers that plant something and something grows from it.
6. The test was easy, enjoyable.
7. He gave her many gifts, like the water from a shower.

p. 50 — Day 9:
1. comitted   2. safetey   3. reletive
4. wheather   5. personel   6. wendsday
7. throughn   8. agread   9. arithmatic
10. breakfest 11. Feburary 12. animel
13. cieties   14. grieff   15. caried
1. 11/3   2. 23/5   3. 12/7
4. 23/6   5. 31/4   6. 2 1/2
7. 5 6/7   8. 4 4/7   9. 1 4/9
10. 3 1/8

P. 51 — Day 10:
1. Baseball players of different races were not allowed to play in the same leagues
2. Vice President.
3. He would not fight back when confronted with racism
4. Answers will vary – could include positive self image, patience, respect

Use a timer to motivate your child to stay on task and finish their work in a timely manner.

p. 55 — Day 1:
1. 2/3   2. 5/8   3. 10/9 = 11/9
4. 9/7 = 12/7   5. 6/27= 2/9
6. 6/20 = 3/10   7. 2/5   8. 5/15 = 1/3
9. 15/19   10. 21/15 = 16/15 = 12/5
1. tunnel and moat
2. wanted to enjoy their fort
3. falling apart
4. boards, nails, hammers
5. Answers will vary

p. 56 — Day 1:
1. yourself   2. myself   3. itself
4. themselves 5. herself 6. ourselves
7. himself   8. ourselves 9. yourselves
10. ourselves
Science – no answer needed

p. 57 — Day 2:
1. 1/18   2. 59/40 = 119/40   3. 5/24
4. 19/27   5. 7/30   6. 17/18
1. peasants
2. knights protected lords; lords gave knights land
3. servant

p. 58 — Day 2:
1. through   2. waste   3. holes
4. their   5. wait   6. sale
7. which   8. weather   9. fourth
10. they're   11. whole   12. there
13. weight   14. whether
15. threw Water cycle diagrams will vary. Check online.

p. 59 —Day 3:
1. N   2. Y   3. Y   4. N   5. Y

p. 60 — Day 3:
1. as well as 2. however   3. first, then
4. but   5. instead of 6. first, then
7. because of   8. To summarize
9. in addition   10. together with
11. although 12. Despite   13. in case of
14. all things considered
1. 4 1/15   2. 8 34/40 = 8 17/20
3. 8 5/12   4. 814/10 = 9 2/5
5. 2 13/24

p. 61 — Day 4:
Answers will vary

p. 62 — Day 4:
1. is   2. are   3. has
4. say   5. is   6. is
7. remembers 8. wants   9. were
10. play   11. has   12. have
13. is   14. believe
1. 5/30 = 1/6   2. 6/20 = 3/10
3. 35/63 = 5/9   4. 1/15

p. 63 — Day 5:
1. Being poor
2. Owned a real estate office, owned a restaurant, created and marketed a popular dessert
3. 1/4 of her salary
4. The students did well enough in school to graduate from high school. They went on to college and trade schools.

p. 67 — Day 6:
Spices, gold, and information
1. 6/4 = 11/2   2. 8/9   3. 40/5 = 8

p. 68 — Day 6:
1. into the huge garden
2. on the chair
3. according to some people
4. in addition to raking the yard
5. between the flower garden and the little pond
6-9 Answers will vary

p. 69 — Day 7:
1. 6/52 = 3/26   2. 152/12 = 122/3
3. 168/84 = 2   4. 168/108 = 15/9
5. 35/26 = 19/26   6. 60/30 = 2
1. Gravity   2. universe   3. stars
4. orbit, moons   5. atmosphere
6. Earth

p. 70 — Day 7:
Answers will vary

p. 71 — Day 8:
1. 7 : 8   2. 33 : 35
3. 19 : 16   4. 35 : 33
5. 15 : 17 Challenge ratio of boys to girls in 7th grade
1. near rivers
2. Long hours, difficult conditions, little pay

p. 72 — Day 8:
1. D   2. A   3. C   4. B
5. F   6. H   7. E   8. I
9. J   10. G
11. At the last possible moment
12. Take on more than you can handle
13. Get it exactly right
14. Take someone's place
15. Being curious can lead to trouble
16. Relax
17. Very clear, easily understood
18. Took more than you can eat.

Answer Key

p. 73 — Day 9:

1. 75/100 = 150/200; should be circled
2. 15/30 = 25/45
3. 18   4. 8   5. 15   6. 9

Word Search:

m	r	m	s	s	p	a	c	e	s	s
s	n	e	n	r	o	m	p	p	p	u
a	s	t	r	o	n	o	m	y	n	n
t	r	e	s	m	c	s	y	e	a	a
u	a	o	a	s	p	t	r	o	r	r
r	t	r	e	t	i	p	u	j	u	u
n	s	l	r	u	l	s	c	r	e	e
n	e	p	t	u	n	e	r	r	e	y
t	e	v	t	s	u	n	e	v	v	v
n	o	o	m	u	t	u	m	c	r	r

p. 74 — Day 9:

Accept, effect, a lot, weird, than, passed, lose

1. cute   2. peppery   3. screechy
4. best   5 more careful   6. better
7. worse   8. black   9. empty
10. shimmery   11. nine   12. beautiful
13. huge   14. most comfortable
15. blinding

p. 75 — Day 10:

1. After one has died
2. To inspire and encourage young people's interest in space exploration
3. Attitude
4. Danger
5. Answers could include taught school, volunteered in her church, was a girl scout leader.

p. 79 — Day 1:

1. 0.52   2. 0.63   3. 0.75
4. 0.17   5. 1.23   6. 43%
7. 92%   8. 75%   9. 28%
10. 154%
1. False   2. True   3. False
4. False   5. True

p. 80 — Day 1:

1. Bill and Fred   2. girl   3. tree
4. her   5. his   6. this
7. his or her   8. her   9. their
10. his or her

p. 81 — Day 2:

1. 87.5%   2. 76.9%   3. 65%
4. 25%   5. 20%   6. 50%
1. social contract
2. Declaration of Independence

p. 82 — Day 2:

1. You can understand the utter abandon with which I place my trust in this Nautilus, since I'm its captain, builder, and engineer all in one!
2. Any two: no structural deformities, no rigging to be worn out, no sails, no fires, won't run out of coal, no collisions, no storms
3. A few meters below the waves it is utterly tranquil.

p. 83 — Day 3:

1. 18 ft.   2. 12 ft.   3. 21 ft.
4. 27 ft.   5. 24 ft.
Answers will vary

p. 84 — Day 3:

1. who   2. whom   3. whom
4. whom   5. who   6. whom
7. who   8. whomever
9. who   10. who   11. whom
12. whom   13. whom   14. whom

p. 85 — Day 4:

1. 5:00 PM   2. Saturday 5:00 PM
3. answers vary: payday, people off work, weekend
4. Wednesday 9:00 PM
1. nobles   2. Third Estate
3. First and Second Estate

p. 86 — Day 4:

1. true   2. false   3. true
4. false   5. false   6. true
7. true   8. false

p. 87 — Day 5:

1. He was a farmer, fought in World War I, owned a men's clothing store
2. Honesty and efficiency
3. To begin something; to put into action
4. Worked to provide equality and quality of life for the poor, the elderly, and those discriminated against because of their race

p. 91 — Day 6:

1. 14   2. 7   3. 11   4. -3
5. -9   6. 2   7. 3   8. -2
Answers will vary

p. 92 — Day 6:

1. not extreme, mild
2. rough winds, too hot
3. Thy eternal summer shall not fade
4. Death

p. 93 — Day 7:

1. -21   2. -25   3. 57   4. -8
5. 2   6. -36   7. -2   8. 10
9. -2   10. 7   11. -9   12. 21
13. 1   14. -1
Science – no answer

p. 94 — Day 7:

1. little known
2. scale of notes, notes worth multiples of two, notes must add to the correct number of beats
3. how it is made and how to repair
4. Answers will vary

p. 95 — Day 8:

1. 16   2. -24   3. -30   4. 56
5. -18   6. 35   7. -32   8. 63
9. -6   10. -9   11. 9   12. 6
13. -6   14. -13   15. 9   16. 8
1. Italy, Germany, Austria
2. Serbian killed the Austrian heir

p. 96 — Day 8:

1. A soliloquy is one person talking; a dialogue is two people.
2. She has fallen a long way.
3. She wants to know what he's late for. Another answer is that there's no rule that says she can't follow him.
4. Rabbit holes are dark.
5. Herself
6. She is falling a long way, building up speed.

p. 97 — Day 9:

1. -1.6   2. 0.7   3. -1
4. 39.05   5. Answers will vary

Have your child correct their own work while you read off the answers. This will reinforce the skills they just practiced.

Answer Key

Give your student an opportunity to rework missed questions. Go over any mistakes made together.

Summer Fit Book Report I

Title: _____

Author: _____

Illustrator: _____

Setting (Where the story takes place): _____

Main Character(s):

_____

_____

_____

Write your favorite part of the story
(use separate sheet of paper if needed):

_____

_____

_____

_____

_____

_____

_____

_____

_____

_____

Tell your favorite part of the story to a parent, guardian or friend.

Read a variety of books on topics that interest you already and new areas that you want to explore!

6-7 • © Summer Fit Activities™

Summer Fit Book Report II

Title: _____

Author: _____

Illustrator: _____

Setting (Where the story takes place): _____

Main Character(s):

_____

_____

Write your favorite part of the story
(use separate sheet of paper if needed):

_____

_____

_____

_____

_____

_____

_____

_____

_____

Tell your favorite part of the story to a parent, guardian or friend.

Read a variety of books on topics that interest you already and new areas that you want to explore!

Summer Fit Book Report III

Title: _____

Author: _____

Illustrator: _____

Setting (Where the story takes place): _____

Main Character(s):

_____

_____

_____

Write your favorite part of the story
(use separate sheet of paper if needed):

_____

_____

_____

_____

_____

_____

_____

_____

_____

_____

Tell your favorite part of the story to a parent, guardian or friend.

Read a variety of books on topics that interest you already and new areas that you want to explore!

Summer Fit Book Report IV

Title: _____

Author: _____

Illustrator: _____

Setting (Where the story takes place): _____

Main Character(s):

_____

_____

_____

Write your favorite part of the story
(use separate sheet of paper if needed):

_____

_____

_____

_____

_____

_____

_____

_____

_____

_____

Tell your favorite part of the story to a parent, guardian or friend.

Read a variety of books on topics that interest you already and new areas that you want to explore!

HEALTH & NUTRITION

6-7 • © Summer Fit Activities™

Let's Play

There are so many ways to play! Check off the different activities as you play them, have fun!

Everybody has different abilities and interests, so take the time to figure out what activities and exercises you like. Try them all: soccer, dance, karate, basketball and skating are only a few. After you have played a lot of different ones, go back and focus on the ones you like! Create your own ways to be active and combine different activities and sports to put your own twist on things. Talk with your parents or caregiver for ideas and have them help you find and do the activities that you like best. Playing and exercising is a great way to help you become fit, but remember that the most important thing about playing is that you are having fun!

List of Exercise Activities

Home–Outdoor:

Walking
Ride Bicycle
Swimming
Walk Dog
Golf with whiffle balls outside
Neighborhood walks/Exploring
(in a safe area)
Hula Hooping
Rollerskating/Rollerblading
Skateboarding
Jump rope
Climbing trees
Play in the back yard
Hopscotch
Stretching
Basketball
Yard work
Housecleaning

Home – Indoor:

Dancing
Exercise DVD
Yoga DVD
Home gym equipment
Stretch bands
Free weights
Stretching

With friends or family:

Red Rover
Chinese jump rope
Regular jump rope
Ring around the rosie
Tag/Freeze
Four score
Capture the flag
Dodgeball
Slip n Slide
Wallball
Tug of War
Stretching
Run through a sprinkler
Skipping
Family swim time
Bowling
Basketball
Hiking
Red light, Green light
Kick ball
Four Square
Tennis
Frisbee
Soccer
Jump Rope
Baseball

Turn off TV Go Outside - PLAY!
Public Service Announcement Brought to you by Summer Fit

Chill out on Screen Time

Screen time is the amount of time spent watching TV, DVDs or going to the movies, playing video games, texting on the phone and using the computer. The more time you spend looking at a screen the less time you are outside riding your bike, walking, swimming or playing soccer with your friends. Try to spend no more than a couple hours a day in front of a screen for activities other than homework and get outside and play!

6-7 • © Summer Fit Activities™

HEALTHY BODIES

There are many ways to enrich your life by eating healthy, exercising each day and playing! Keeping your body strong and healthy will help you feel good and even perform better in school. To be healthy, you need to eat right, get enough sleep and exercise. What you learn and do with Summer Fit Activities™ is just the beginning. From here, you will be able to find other healthy and active things to do based on your interests, abilities and personal goals.

 Aerobic Exercises help your cardiovascular system that includes your heart and blood vessels. You need a strong heart to pump blood. Your blood delivers oxygen and nutrients to your body.

 Strength Exercises help you make your muscles stronger and increase your muscular endurance. Endurance helps you get the most from your muscles before you get tired!!

 Flexibility Exercises are good for many reasons including warming up before you do aerobic or strength exercises. Flexibility also helps you use all your muscles in different ways, positions and ranges of motion.

Your body composition is made up of lean mass and fat mass. Lean mass includes water, muscles and organs in your body. Fat mass includes fat your body needs for later and stores for energy.

Exercise helps you burn body fat and do more of the activities you want to do like hiking, biking and playing at the beach. There are a lot fun sports and activities to choose from that will help you strengthen your body and your brain!

Get Active!

Apple	Brain
Water	Vegetable
Exercise	Muscles
Aerobic	Organs
Strength	Fun
Flexibility	Play

```
D G L H B J S Z V Z B R F P C
Y H V T T E V E V A Z Y L F I
A C U P L G G M Y K I V E S B
G O T C A E N G H T P W X M O
H E S X T L M E Y A L P I L R
A U Y A E S I C R E X E B V E
M P B Y B M R G B T H Z I Q A
I L P R O L S V V F S R L K X
E Y A L D P E N B G A R I I I
F I B P E L H Y U V I F T W N
N G T D J A U D L F Z Q Y A X
O N M C X A V R S I V J S T J
O R G A N S B W A K K R A E C
J T C E L Y R C U Z R B G R P
X J P Y A W W E O S C K I K J
```

Active Lifestyle Pop Quiz!

What does being active mean to you?

List your 3 favorite aerobic activities

1) _____

2) _____

3) _____

EX:

bicycling, running, swimming, skateboarding, hiking

List 2 sports you like to play

1) _____

2) _____

EX:

lacrosse, basketball, baseball, dance, volleyball

List 3 activities you like that help build strength and flexibility

1) _____

2) _____

3) _____

EX:

yoga, dance, gymnastics, martial arts, jump rope

List 3 fun things you like to do that get you moving

1) _____

2) _____

3) _____

EX:

bowling, skating, fishing, gardening, cooking

List 2 things you can limit that will help you be more active:

1) _____

2) _____

EX:

video games, TV, phone

List 3 things you can do to help the environment and get you moving more often!

1) _____

2) _____

3) _____

EX:

pick up trash in neighborhood, separate items in recycling bins, help plant a garden, wash your water cup and reuse, ride your bike

6-7 • © Summer Fit Activities™

Summer Fitness Program

The goal of your Summer Fitness program is to help you improve in all areas of physical fitness and to be active every day.

You build cardiovascular endurance through aerobic exercise. For aerobic exercise, you need to work large muscle groups that get your heart pumping and oxygen moving through your entire body. This increases your heart rate and breathing. On your aerobic day, you can jog, swim, hike, dance, skateboard, ride your bike, roller blade... there are so many to choose from

Your goal should be to try to get 30 minutes a day of aerobic exercise at least 2-3 times a week. Follow your daily Summer Fit™ exercise schedule and choose your own aerobic exercises along the way.

You build your muscular strength and muscle endurance with exercises that work your muscles, like push-ups, sit-ups and pull-ups. Increase how many you can do of each of these over time and pay attention to your Summer Fit ™daily exercises for other activities that help build strong muscles.

Get loose – stretch. Warming up before you exercise if very important. It prepares your body for exercising by loosening your muscles and getting your body ready for training. An easy start is to shake your arms and roll your shoulders!

Time to Hydrate

It is important to drink water before and after you exercise because water regulates your body temperature and gives you nutrients to keep you healthy.

The next time you exercise, drink a cup of water before and after you are done.

Color the bottom half of the cup red below to represent the water you drink before you exercise. Color the top half of the cup blue to represent the water you drink after you exercise.

Water Facts

There is the same amount of water on earth today as there was when dinosaurs roamed through our backyards!

75% of your brain is water!

Water regulates the earth's temperature.

Water is made up of two elements, hydrogen and oxygen. Its chemical formula is H_2O

Water is essential for life on earth.

Here are instructions for your daily exercises. Talk with a parent about setting goals. Set your goals for time or reps. Keep track of your goals using your Summer Fitness Chart. Have fun!

Aerobic Exercises and Activities

Jogging in Place: Run slowly in place or outside to accomplish your time goal.

Bump and Jump: Jump forward and back, jump side to side. Hop on one foot to another, moving side-to-side, alternating feet. Quicken your pace.

Let's Dance: Step to your right with your right foot (putting your weight on your right foot). Step behind your right foot with your left foot (putting your weight on your left foot). Step again to the right with your right foot (weight on right) and touch your left foot next to your right (with your weight staying on the right foot). Repeat the above going left but switching to the other foot.
Goal = Dance for 5 minutes
Do the Cha-cha Step forward right, cha-cha Step forward left, cha-cha Repeat
Do the Cross over Cross right over left, kick out right leg then backwards cha-cha-cha Cross left over right, kick out left leg then backwards cha-cha-cha Repeat
Do the Rope Rope 1/4 to the left 1/4 facing the rear 1/4 turn left again Rope to the front and step together with a clap. Repeat (When you "rope" hold one hand above your head and swing your arms in a circle like you have a rope above you).

Pass and Go: This activity requires a second person. Ask a friend or someone from your family to play with you. The object of this activity is to pass a ball back and forth counting by 2's get to a 100 as fast as you can. Have a stopwatch handy. Set a time you want to beat and go! Increase your goal by setting a lower time. Repeat.

Step It Up: This activity uses stairs if you have them. If you do, take three trips up and down the stairs. Raise your legs high like you are in a marching band. If you do not have stairs, do 20 step-ups on one step. Start slow and increase your speed.

Kangaroo Bounce: Tape a shoelace to the floor in a straight line. Stand on one side of the string with both feet together. Jump forward over the string and then backward to land in your original place. Take a short break—and do it again. This time jump side-to-side over the shoelace.

Garbage Hoops: A trashcan makes a great indoor basketball goal— perfect for a quick game of one-on-one against yourself or a friend! Use a bottle-cap or crunched up ball of paper as your basketball. Twist, jump and make sure to use a few fakes to win the game! First one to 11 wins!

Green Giant: Mow the grass, weed the garden or pick up your yard. Feeling good today? Mow your neighbors yard too!

Capture the Flag: Use scarves or old T-shirts for flags. Assign a different color one for each team. Use chalk, cones, tape, or landmarks such as trees or sidewalks to divide your playing area into equal-sized territories for each team. Place one flag into each territory. It must be visible and once it is placed it cannot be moved. When the game begins, players cross into opposing teams' territories to grab their flags. When a player is in an opposing team's territory they can be captured by the other team. Once they are tagged he/she must run to the sideline and perform an exercise—for example, five jumping jacks or three push-ups. After they perform their exercise the player can go back to their team territory and resume play. The game ends when one team successfully captures the flag(s) from the other team or teams and returns to their own territory with the opposing team's flag.

Happy Feet: Use your feet every chance you get today. Walk to a friend's house, to the store, around the park or wherever it's safe to walk. Get your parents to walk with you after dinner.

Let's Roll: Put your lungs to work on your bike, skates or scooter. Don't forget to wear helmets and pads!

Speed: Walk a block, than run as fast as you can the next block. Alternate between walking and running blocks. Rest in between. Time yourself and see if you can beat your original time. Repeat. **Goal = 2 blocks**

Tag: Decide who is "IT." Choose the boundaries for the game. If a player crosses the boundaries during the game, he/she is automatically "IT."
Give players a 15 second head start. "IT" counts to 15 and then chases the others to tag them! The player who has been tagged is now "IT!"

Hide and Seek: Select an area to play. Designate a specific area with clear boundaries. Have everyone gather around a tree or other landmark, which is "home base." Whoever goes first must close his/her eyes and count to 10. Everybody else hides during the count. After the count is over, call out "Ready or not here I come!" Now it's time to look for the other players who are hiding. They are trying to get to home base before they are found. If they get to home base without being found they are "safe." The first player found loses and they start the next game by counting to 10!

Hula-Hoop: Hold the hula-hoop around your waist with both hands. Pull it forward so it is resting against your back. With both hands, fling the hoop to the left so that rolls in a circle around your body. Do this a few times until you get the feel of it. Leave the hula-hoop on the ground for a few minutes and practice swirling your hip. Move your pelvis left, back, right, forward. Find a groove and keep the hoop going around your hips as long as you can. When it falls to the ground pick it up and try again!

Jump Rope: Start by holding an end of the rope in each hand. Position the rope behind you on the ground. Raise your arms up and turn the rope over your head bringing it down in front of you. When it reaches the ground, jump over it. Find a good pace, not too slow and not too fast. Jump over the rope each time it comes around. Continue until you reach your goal of jumping a certain amount of times without stopping.

Strength Exercises and Activities

Knee lifts: Stand with your feet flat on the floor. Start by lifting your right knee up 5 times, always bring both feet together between each interval then change legs. When you feel more confident, bounce while you bring your knee up and alternate between legs.

Pushups: Start in an elevated position. Keep your body straight, head facing forward. Lower yourself down by bending your elbows. Once your chest touches the ground, push back up to your starting position.

Curl-ups: Start by lying on the floor, knees bent and arms crossed in front. Rise up and forward until your chest touches your raised knee. As soon as you touch your knee, go back down slowly to your starting position.

Squats: Stand up straight with your legs shoulder width apart. Keep your ankles and legs pointed straight forward. Raise your arms in front of you during the exercise. Bend your knees and lower yourself down like you are going to sit in a chair until your bottom is in a straight line with your knees while keeping your back straight. If you cannot make it down this far, go as far as you can, hold for two seconds and slowly raise back up to your starting position.

Chop n Squat: Start with legs wide, bring your feet together, then out wide again, reach down and touch the ground, and pop up.

Chin Ups: Start by hanging from the bar with your arms fully extended, keeping your feet off the ground. Your hands should be facing into the bar with your palms on the bar itself. Pull yourself up until your chin touches the bar. When you touch the bar with your chin, slowly let yourself down to your starting position and repeat the exercise.

Leg Raise: Lie on your back with your legs straight in the air forming a 90- degree angle. Lower your legs downward, stopping a few inches from the ground. Pause, and return to your starting position. Keep your back flat on the floor the entire time.

Balance: Balance on one foot. Foot extended low in front of you. Foot extended low in back of you. Foot extended low to the side.

Jumping Jacks: Jump to a position with your legs spread wide and your hands touching overhead and then returning to a position with your feet together and arms at your sides. A more intense version is to bend down (over) and touch the floor in between each jump.

Shoulder Rolls: Place your arms at your side while standing at attention. Lift your shoulders into an "up" position and roll them forward while pulling into your chest.

Lunges: Stand straight with your legs shoulder width apart. Keep your hands at your side. Step forward with one leg, bending at your knee to lower your body. Move back into your starting position and repeat. Alternate between legs after performing a number of reps.

Heel Raises: Stand on the floor with your feet pointing forward and about one foot apart. Keep your knees straight, but do not lock them into place. Raise yourself up onto the balls of your feet and squeeze your calf muscle. Hold this position before releasing back into your starting position.

Chair Dips: Sit in a chair with your hands placed firmly on the arms of the chair. Extend your legs out so they are resting on your heels. Lift your bottom up from the chair by extending your arms straight up. Lower yourself down by bending your elbows into a 90-degree angle. Do not let your bottom touch the chair. Push back up and repeat the exercise.

Crisscross: Lie on your back with your shoulders 3-5 inches off the ground and your heels raised off the floor. Keep your mid and lower sections of your back flat on the floor and keep your abdominal muscles tight. Rest your arms next to you on the floor. Cross your left foot over the right foot. Without stopping, rotate your feet so the right is over your left foot. Continue this pattern without resting.

Scissors: Lie on your back with your shoulders 3-5 inches off the ground and your heels raised off the floor. Raise your legs 3-5 more inches higher while keeping your legs straight. Alternate between legs so you are creating a scissor motion with your legs going up and down opposite each other.

Floor Bridge: Lie down on your back with your knees bent, feet flat on the floor. Rest your arms at your sides, palms down. Draw your belly in and push through your heels to lift your pelvis off the floor. Slowly lower your hips and pelvis back to the floor.

Leg Crab Kick: Get into a crab walk position by lying on your back and extending your arms and your legs up so you are supporting yourself with your hands and feet. Once your bottom is in the air, kick out with your right leg. Bring the right leg back and kick out with your left leg. Alternate between legs.

Air Jump Rope: Jump up and down while moving your arms in a circular motion as if you were swinging a jump rope.

Chest Touch Pushups: Start in an elevated position with your arms holding you up. Keep your body straight, head facing forward. Lower yourself towards the ground with both arms. Once your chest touches the ground start pushing back up to your starting position, while touching the left side of your chest with your right hand. Once completed drop your right arm down to the ground so you are holding yourself up with both arms in your starting position. Repeat the exercise, this time touching the right side of your chest with your left arm. Alternate between left and right.

Plank: Lie face down while resting on your forearms with your feet together. Sweep the floor with your arms to separate your shoulders and tuck your chin, creating a straight line from the top of your head to your heels. Hold this position.

Side Step: Lunge out to your right. Back leg straight, bend the right knee. Slide back and bend the left knee and straighten the right leg. Turn and face the opposite direction and repeat.

Mountain Climbers: Start in your pushup position. Then lift one leg a few inches off the ground and pull it up towards your chest. Hold your knee tucked in for 2 seconds, then return to your start position. Alternate legs like you are climbing up a mountain.

Toe Taps: Start by standing with your two feet shoulder length apart with your back straight and your arms by your sides. While jumping straight up, bring one toe forward to the front and tap while alternating to the opposite foot. Go back and forth between your left and right foot. Find a rhythm and be careful not to lose your balance!

NUTRITION

Hey Parents!

A healthy diet and daily exercise will maximize the likelihood of your child growing up healthy and strong. Children are constantly growing and adding bone and muscle mass, so a balanced diet is very important to their overall health. Try to provide three nutritious meals a day that all include fruits and vegetables. Try to limit fast food and cook at home as often as you can. Not only is it better on your pocketbook, cooking at home is better for you and can be done together as a family. Everyone can help and it is more likely you will eat together as a family.

As a healthy eating goal, avoid food and drinks that are high in sugar as much as possible. Provide fresh fruits, vegetables, grains, lean meats, chicken, fish and low-fat dairy items as much as possible.

5 Steps to Improve Eating Habits

 Make fresh fruits and vegetables readily available

 Cook more at home, and sit down for dinner as a family.

 Limit sugary drinks, cereals and desserts

 Serve smaller portions

 Limit snacks to 1 or 2 daily

HEALTHY EATING POP QUIZ!

What does eating
healthy mean to <u>you</u>?

List your 3 favorite healthy foods:

1) _____   2) _____   3) _____

If you were only to eat vegetables,
what 5 vegetables would you choose?

1) _____   2) _____

3) _____   4) _____   5) _____

Fill in the names of 5 different food groups on the Food Plate.

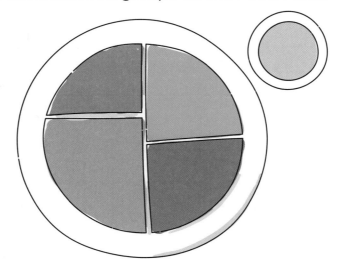

Circle the food and drink items that are healthy foods from the list below:

Milk	*Apple*	*Chicken*	*Salad*
candy	*butter*	*soda*	*orange*
ice cream	*carrot*	*cotton candy*	*chocolate shake*

List your 3 favorite healthy foods

1) _____   2) _____   3) _____

Create a list of foods you would like to grow in a garden

Nutrition – *Food Plate*

It is important to eat different foods from the 5 different food groups. Eating a variety of foods helps you stay healthy. Some foods give you protein and fats. Other foods give you vitamins, minerals and carbohydrates. Your body needs all of these to grow healthy and strong!

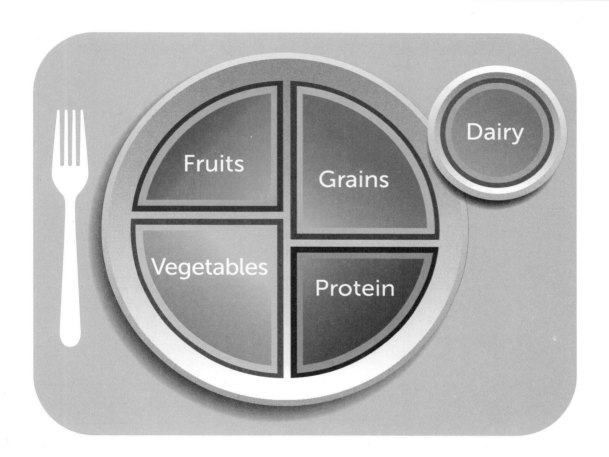

List 3 different foods for each category.

Fruits	Vegetables	Grains	Protein	Dairy
1) _____	1) _____	1) _____	1) _____	1) _____
2) _____	2) _____	2) _____	2) _____	2) _____
3) _____	3) _____	3) _____	3) _____	3) _____

Nutrition – *Meal Planner*

Plan out 3 balanced meals for one day.
Organize your meals so you will eat all the
recommended foods listed on the Food Plate.

BREAKFAST

LUNCH

DINNER

Nutrition – *Meal Tracker*

Use these charts to list the different foods from the different food categories on My Plate that you eat each day.
Every day you mark each food category color in the vegetable!

	Grains	Dairy	Protein	Fruits	Vegetables	
Monday						
Tuesday						
Wednesday						
Thursday						
Friday						
Saturday						
Sunday						

	Grains	Dairy	Protein	Fruits	Vegetables	
Monday						
Tuesday						
Wednesday						
Thursday						
Friday						
Saturday						
Sunday						

MY OWN HEALTHY SNACKS

Frozen Banana Slices

Prep Time: 10 minutes

Freezer Time: 2 hours

Yield: 2 servings, Good for all ages!

Ingredients: 2 fresh bananas

Directions: Peel the bananas and cut them into 5-6 slices each. Place the banana slices on a plate and place in freezer for 2 hours. Enjoy your frozen banana snack on a hot summer day!

Yogurt Parfaits

Prep Time: 15 minutes

Cook Time: 0 minutes

Yield: 4 servings, Good for all ages!

Ingredients: 2 cups fresh fruit, at least 2 different kinds (can also be thawed fresh fruit)
1 cup low-fat plain or soy yogurt
4 TBSP 100% fruit spread
1 cup granola or dry cereal

Directions: Wash and cut fruit into small pieces. In a bowl, mix the yogurt and fruit spread together. Layer each of the four parfaits as follows: Fruit Yogurt Granola (repeat) Enjoy!

Frozen Grapes

Prep Time: 10 minutes

Freezer Time: 2 hours

Yield: 4 servings, Good for all ages!

Ingredients: Seedless grapes

Directions: Wash seedless grapes and separate them from their stem. Place into a bowl or plastic bag. Put them into the freezer for 2 hours. Enjoy your cold, sweet and crunchy treat!

Fruit Smoothies

Prep Time: 5 minutes

Cook Time: 0 minutes

Yield: 2 servings, Good for all ages!

Ingredients: 1 cup berries, fresh or frozen
4 ounces Greek yogurt
1/2 cup 100% apple juice
1 banana, cut into chunks
4 ice cubes

Directions: Place apple juice, yogurt, berries and banana into blender. Cover and blend until smooth. While the blender is running, drop ice cubes into the blender one at a time. Blend until smooth. Pour and enjoy!

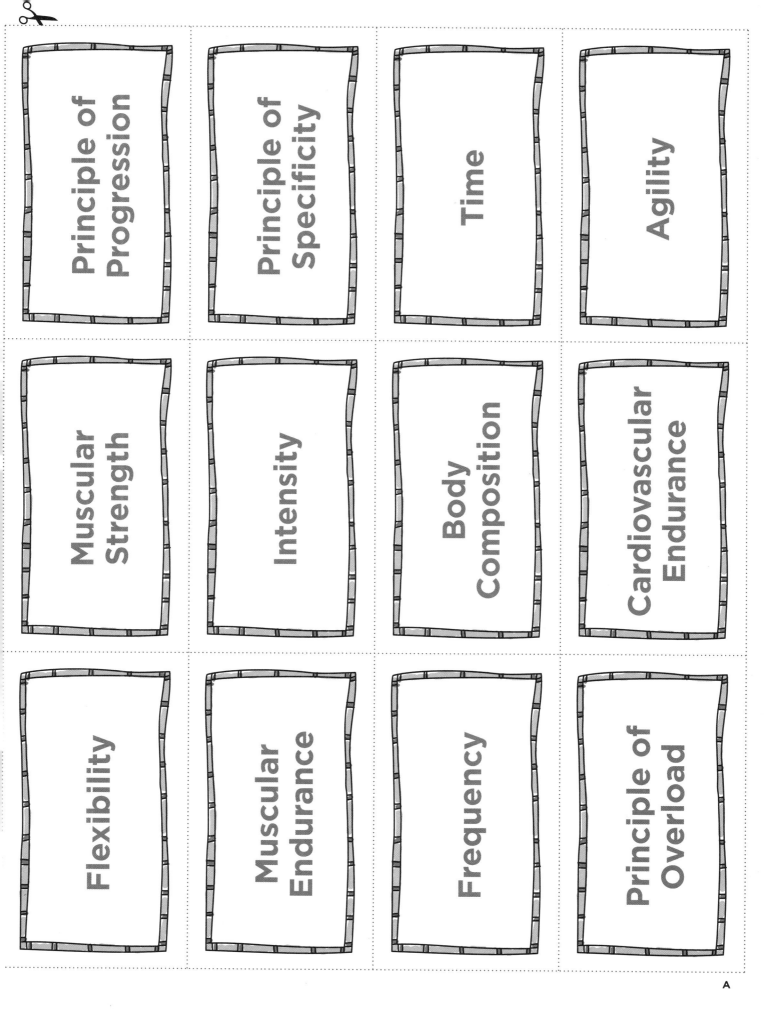

Principle of Progression

Principle of Specificity

Time

Agility

Muscular Strength

Intensity

Body Composition

Cardiovascular Endurance

Flexibility

Muscular Endurance

Frequency

Principle of Overload

A

Ability to change the position of your body while maintaining control

How long you participate in physical activity

The exercise you do, determines the benefit you receive

Increase your exercise gradually

How long you exercise without stopping

Ratio of fat tissue to lean tissue — different for everybody

How hard you work during physical activity

Ability to use your muscles to produce force

Your body must work more than normal while you exercise

How often you participate in physical activity

How long you can use your muscles without tiring

Ability to move joints in a wide range of motions

B

c

D

spend

experiment

touch

drop

appear

ate

dinner

hurt

speech

forth

nation

knowledge

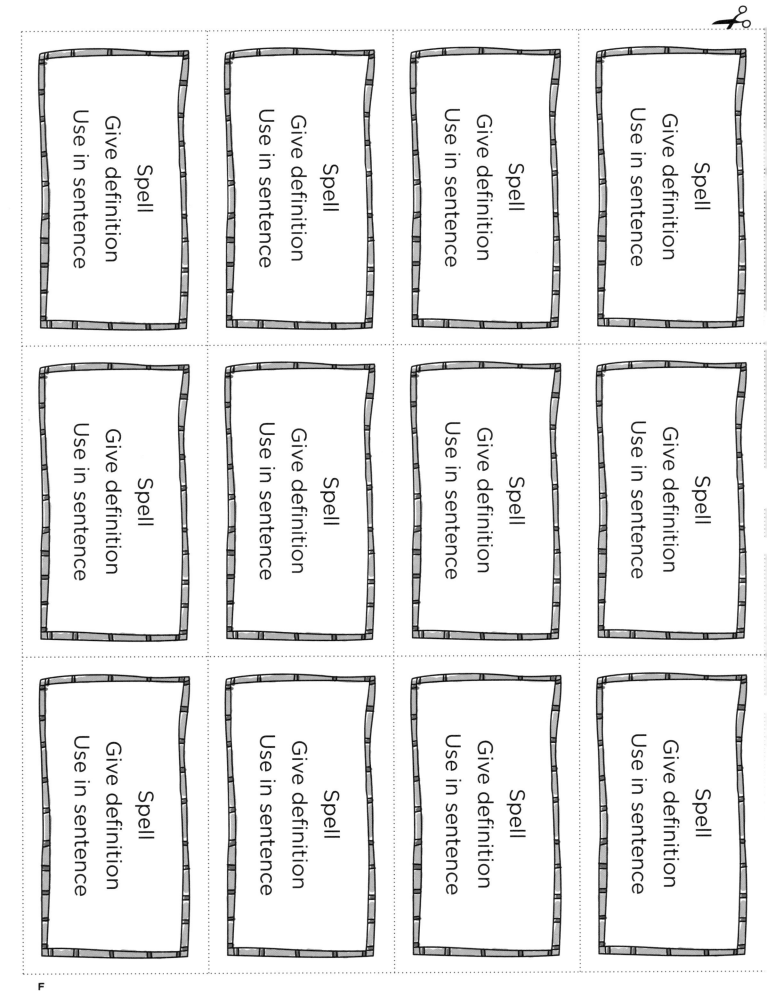

Spell
Give definition
Use in sentence

Spell
Give definition
Use in sentence

Spell
Give definition
Use in sentence

Spell
Give definition
Use in sentence

Spell
Give definition
Use in sentence

Spell
Give definition
Use in sentence

Spell
Give definition
Use in sentence

Spell
Give definition
Use in sentence

Spell
Give definition
Use in sentence

Spell
Give definition
Use in sentence

Spell
Give definition
Use in sentence

Spell
Give definition
Use in sentence

F

shop

unless

spot

neither

sing

column

twice

particular

chair

east

separate

truck

G

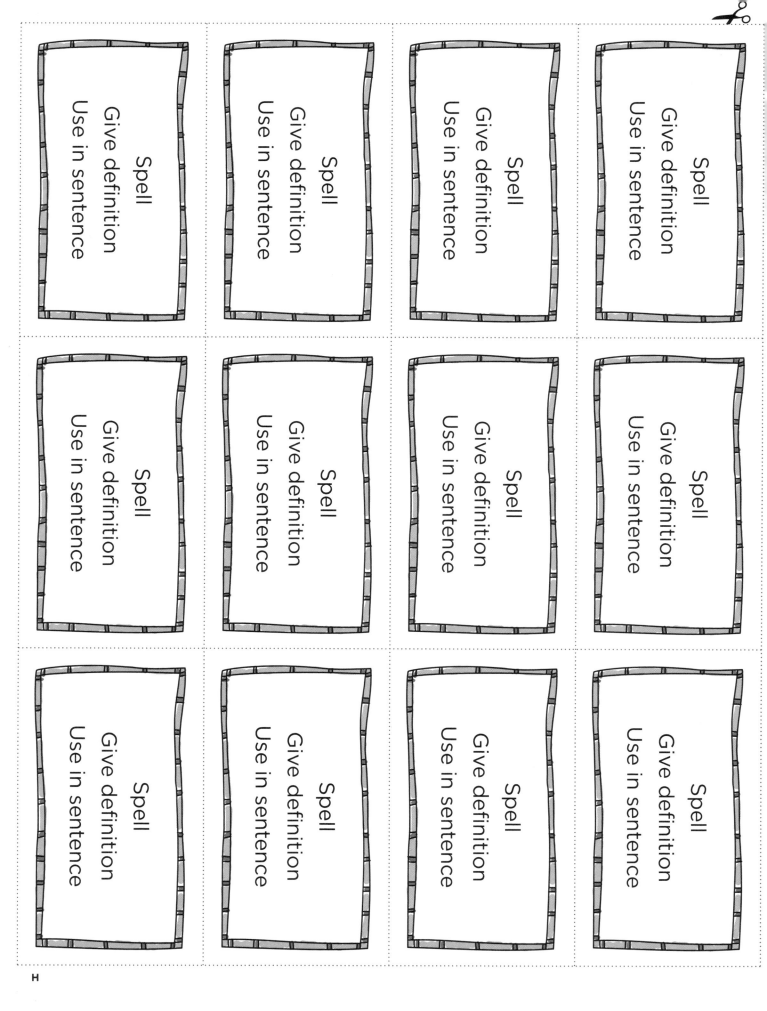

Spell
Give definition
Use in sentence

Spell
Give definition
Use in sentence

Spell
Give definition
Use in sentence

Spell
Give definition
Use in sentence

Spell
Give definition
Use in sentence

Spell
Give definition
Use in sentence

Spell
Give definition
Use in sentence

Spell
Give definition
Use in sentence

Spell
Give definition
Use in sentence

Spell
Give definition
Use in sentence

Spell
Give definition
Use in sentence

Spell
Give definition
Use in sentence

J

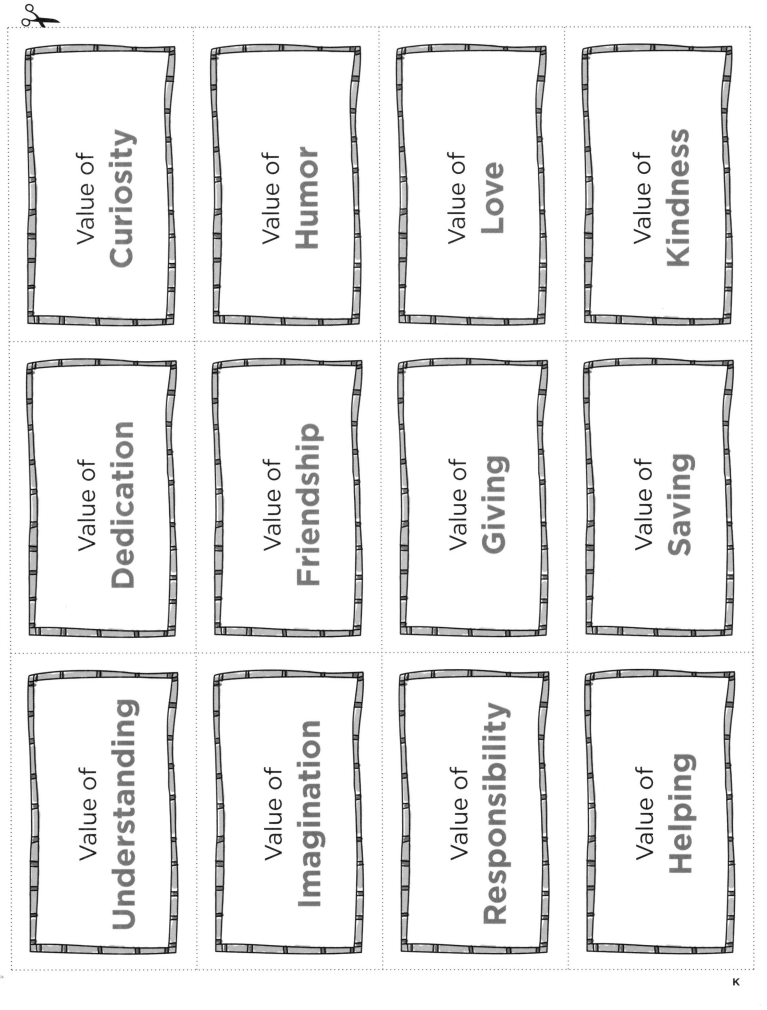

Value of **Curiosity**

Value of **Humor**

Value of **Love**

Value of **Kindness**

Value of **Dedication**

Value of **Friendship**

Value of **Giving**

Value of **Saving**

Value of **Understanding**

Value of **Imagination**

Value of **Responsibility**

Value of **Helping**

K

Desire to know or learn something

Positive state of mind, being funny

Deep affection and caring for another person

Being friendly, generous, considerate

To be committed to a task or purpose

Mutual trust and support between people

To offer or hand over something

Preventing the waste of something

Aware of, and interested in learning other people, ideas and beliefs

Ability to be creative and resourceful

Being accountable for your actions and other peoples

To contribute and offer assistance

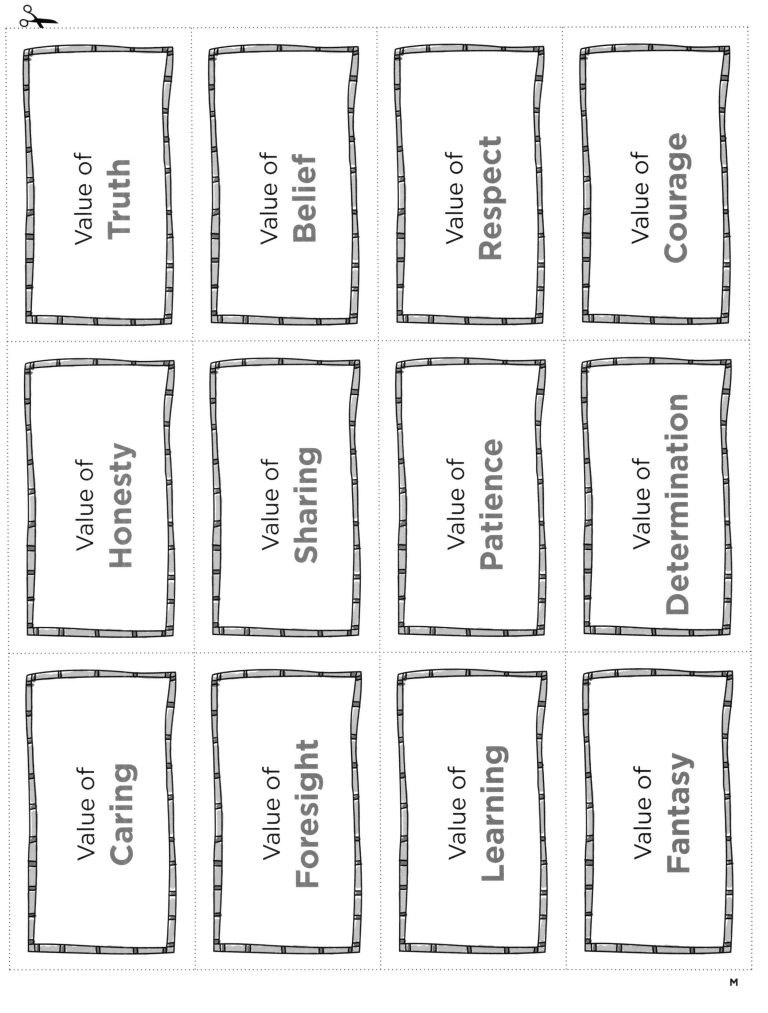

Value of **Truth**

Value of **Belief**

Value of **Respect**

Value of **Courage**

Value of **Honesty**

Value of **Sharing**

Value of **Patience**

Value of **Determination**

Value of **Caring**

Value of **Foresight**

Value of **Learning**

Value of **Fantasy**

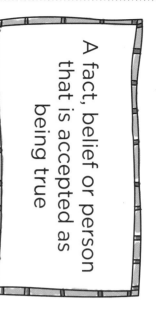

A fact, belief or person that is accepted as being true

Trust, faith or confidence in someone or something

Admire someone for their abilities, qualities or achievements

Ability to do something that frightens you

Sincere, free of deceit

To give to others

Accept or tolerate without getting upset

Being resolute to an idea or purpose

Displaying kindness and concern for others

Being able to predict needs or what will happen in the future

Knowledge through experience, study or being taught

Being able to imagine the impossible